I0565151

Girl, Get Up and Win!

Compiled by *Telishia Berry*

Publisher of *Courageous Woman Magazine*

ISBN-13: 978-0-9786001-3-6

Strive Publishing is a division of Courageous Media Group. For more information on the authors, ordering, book signings, or to sponsor an event, contact us at: info@courageouswomanmag.com

Edited/formatted by Shonell Bacon

Cover designed by Oladimeji Basit Alaka

Dedication

This book is dedicated to the many women who are dealing with traumatic life issues and need inspiration, to the many courageous women in our network who have shared their stories of courage, to the women who have shared their stories in this book, and to the many women these writers have and will continue to inspire.

Thank you all.

Together, we will help heal women around the world.

Contents

Acknowledgments

To my daughters Kennedy, Toya, Tisha, and my son, Kendre', you have witnessed me overcome so much. I hope my life and my work will inspire you to always have hope and believe that you can get through and overcome any challenges you may face and win, no matter what!

To all my aunties, cousins, besties, sisters, women in Christ, women warriors, and the many courageous women and men who have stood with me, prayed for me, counseled me, and led me to into courageousness, **THANK YOU!**

To my editor Shonell Bacon and editorial manager Dr. Ladel Lewis, thank you for being on my team and for having my back!

Introduction

From childhood to adulthood, as a woman, a mother, a wife-to-ex-wife, a daughter, sister, and friend, I have endured many challenges; some were harder than others, and some were out right tragic, but by the grace of God, I made it through!

Stories about women overcoming challenges, succeeding in business, and surviving tragedies often offer inspiration and hope and belief that if someone else can get through their issues they can, too.

In 2011, I dealt with some life challenges and needed some motivation. I searched the Internet for inspirational readings and couldn't find many stories that related to my personal circumstances, so I decided to create a blog to share inspirational stories

1

about women. Those stories set the tone of the Courageous Woman brand, and soon, we relaunched as a magazine that highlights extraordinary women in business and entertainment.

We have extended our publishing genre to include books. *Girl, Get Up and Win* is a literary expression of hope. I am pleased to present these 40 authors, including a husband and wife team who share heartfelt stories and intimate details about their lives and how they triumphed over their situations. My hope is that these stories will serve as part of the healing process for many and the motivation to proceed forward, to take leaps of faith, to let go of the past, to forgive and, ultimately, to Get Up and Win!

I hope you will read these stories and then share and bless others with this book!

Telishia Berry

Foreword

As an overcomer, it is an honor to express my gratitude to Telishia Berry for asking me to write the foreword for this book. I am also grateful that she had the assignment to share her platform with so many other women who are now overcomers. She is indeed a God ordained midwife being used in this hour to help many great women and men birth their dreams. She is on a journey to assist others to catapult into the dimension of authorship by sharing her gifts and wisdom to do so.

Girl, Get Up and Win is a must read for those who need to be reminded that their victory was already constructed by God. The word declares that as a child of God we are more than conquerors and overcomers by the blood of the lamb. Thus, this book is one that ignites a mentality of steadfastness after reading the testimonies of those who have overcome. Many times, the issues of life plague people with exhaustion so that they can't see their victory ahead. We struggle in secrecy, thus threatening to abort great assignments. We get beat up and broken down just from living and often adopt a defeated disposition. I myself know this all too well as I am recovering from an injury that occurred when a truck driver in an eighteen wheeler hit me. As an avid Zumba dancer, my once vibrant self and body became tired, weary, depressed, aching, and whipped. Therefore, the need for encouragement was crucial for me to leap over my hurdle. I needed someone to be real with me about their once depressed thoughts to help me get past mine.

However, this book candidly exposes the trials that anchored these writers into their overcoming state. They share with authenticity real struggles of depression, loneliness, discouragement, marital issues, infirmities, fatherly love issues, despair, and much more. They allow us to come into their private history so we the reader can indeed be free from any bonds of hopelessness. They expose what was once shame so shackles can release off of others bound. As a caregiver of a mom who has had three strokes and had been stricken with blindness and once the caregiver of a dad who had six amputations, I can identify with feeling defeated. As a woman who was born cripple and later in life dealt with pre-cancer cells, I can relate to their stories. When there was no one to turn to but God, I had to tell myself, "Girl, Get Up" and come out your pity party. It's time to excel!"

Girl, Get Up and Win reminds us that we can exceed and be the victors regardless of our situations.

Our once stumbling blocks are not the end, and this book encourages the most desolate situation to birth life. It is a book that decrees you are blessed as it says in James 1:12 because you stood the test to receive the crown of life as a result of your love for God. So, I dare you to read every testimony and get up out of any place of despair. It is your time to win and shift as an eagle into greatness, thus soaring above the issues of life. You are a conqueror, and don't forget it as you flip through these pages of victory. Your trials tried to alter your greatness, steal, kill, and destroy you. But your past letdowns do not have to promise you future failures. You are a success story, too, just waiting to be written. After all, Telishia was given this assignment to help you win the race by reading others' victory reports. So, dare to be that winner and obtain all your greatness with Christ!

Apostle Veryl Howard

Girl, Get Up and Win

Overcoming Childhood

Girl, Get Up and Win

Mother–Child Relationship

Jeanette Abney

When it comes to relationships, a child's very first relationship is with their parents. In my case, it was with my mother. My mother met my father at the age of fourteen only to marry at the age of sixteen. And from what I have been told, such was not a very positive or nurturing relationship. It had its ups and downs only to have me become the oldest of such union, which later led to a drastic yet unresolved twist. My mother never wanted people to know who was the father of myself or my siblings, which for years really did not make sense to me, yet I later learned that such did not matter as it was none of my business nor could I do anything about it. My mother carried such to her grave.

For years, I always knew that I was different. I began to realize at an early age that such was the foundation of a mother-child relationship. Not to mention one that began to become the blueprint of my life. Such shaped how I viewed myself, the world, and those around me. I cannot say that it was all bad.

Nor is my mother here to defend herself. My mother was a cold piece of work. And my ultimate goal was to not be anything like her. Such may sound harsh, yet from what I witnessed as a child, I vowed to do things differently if I became a mother, and for years, I always believed that I would be childless, yet I knew that I wanted to have a career.

As a child, I was told that upon birth, my father was told, "We can either save your wife or your child." It was said that my father replied, " Save my wife." My grandmother said, "Save my grandchild." With that being said, such should tell you about how our mother-daughter relationship was. Such appeared to have been a generational curse. It appeared to be dysfunctional. Yet it was love as we both knew it. As I developed into a young adult, I learned what a maternal bond was *supposed* to be between a mother and her child.

Typically, when one thinks about this type of relationship, what comes to mind is unconditional love, emotional attachment, being nurtured, and that is to name a few. But what I learned was that my mother was beautiful, uneducated yet street smart. She was not nurtured as a child herself, depressed, angry, and an alcoholic, yet she was a hard worker, protector, survivor, and was loyal to children, family, and those around her, all qualities that she taught me. The other lessons I did my best to ignore.

My mother and I had a very unique relationship. For years, I always thought that she did not like me. Yet I was her first born and her ride or die. We fought many battles together and often fought against one another. One would say that I was her most challenging and most difficult child because my other sisters feared her. Yet, I felt I was going to survive even at the hands of her.

I recall my mother saying to "Keep living." And even when I had children, she was disappointed in me. When I had my first child, she wanted my son as her own only to ruin him as I later learned that my mother did better with males than she did with females, which as I indicated earlier appeared to had been a generational curse.

With that being said, I can recall as a child being called "Jean's Kid." And if you add the "ette" to "Jean," you would get *Jeanette*. At a very young age, I lost my mother to breast cancer. One of the hardest things that I ever had to do was watch the person that I had known for all of my life to be full of life, feisty, mean-spirited, and, as many have said, gangster lose her life at the age of 59. I felt that I had lost my best friend, comrade, confidant, enemy, and mother at the same time. Our relationship to the world was dysfunctional and unhealthy. Yet I had to learn prior to her death that one can't teach what they do not know. Nor can one give what they do not have. My mother was there for me the best that she could. I learned to appreciate her as the mother she was as she had taught me a lot of good qualities. I later learned how to discern what not to repeat in my life. I learned about the love between a parent and child as well as a mother and daughter. And when I became a mother of a daughter, I wanted to have a different relationship than the one that I had with my mother.

As I think about the subject matter, "Girl Get Up and Win," it makes me think about where I would be if it was not for my mother. Our relationship was far from perfect. However, I learned about the importance of having a strong mother as well as a female protector in my life. I learned that I could not blame my mother for the trials and tribulations in my life. I learned to thank God for having a praying mother that made me go to church even when I did not want to go. I learned to be grateful for the work ethics that she instilled in me as a child. I thought she treated me like a slave as she taught me how to not only do housework, cook, work on cars, and do yard work, and that was before I could go outside and play.

Such has continued to follow me. Now what I had to also learn was to forgive her for what she did not know. I had to learn how to love, show love, and develop healthy relationships with others by not being aggressive or abusive, which is what I witnessed as a child. I had to learn how to let a man be a man. Learn how to trust God and lean not on my own understanding as well as to let another love me. I never struggled with self-esteem issues. Nor have I been a woman that struggled with depression or a drug or alcohol addiction. I recall my mother always saying, "I am not a punk." I'm not either. I have strength beyond measure and a joy that no man can take.

My mother would never settle for second place, and when I think of a winner, I commend her for how she endured her fight with cancer. She never looked sick. Nor did she want people to feel sorry for her. She was a woman of style, beauty, and grace, which are several characters that I came to realize that she instilled in me. I am aware that I am still living off the prayers of my mother.

Interesting as I age, I noticed that I also look a great deal like her. That was something that I had tried to deny practically all of my life. As I learned to develop into a woman, I learned that I am a winner. My life as I grew up in Compton, California, could have went an entirely different route. And that is not to brag but to give honor where honor is due and such is to God and to my mother.

In life, I learned that one can lose yet still be a winner. One can also win yet feel like a loser. When my mother transitioned from this life, as I watched her take her last breath, I realized that I could not take her passing as a loss. I had to embrace it and learn from the experience and look at the situation in a positive way. This year, I became the age that my mother was when she was diagnosed with breast cancer. I was not afraid as I had been told more than once that I had a positive test for breast cancer yet only to be told that it was benign or disappeared.

If you grew up without a mother or perhaps experienced childhood trauma… or perhaps you could have had a dysfunctional relationship with your mother… whether your mother has transitioned or is still on earth, it is not too late to heal. You cannot change another, but you can heal. And when you heal, you will realize that you are a winner despite what others may think.

A Winner's Choice

Mel Robinson

Overcomer, a word I would have never considered using in describing myself. The foundation that established my life had always been consistent in its mixture of two main ingredients, dysfunction and fear. Both began shaping the core of my existence at an early age, and it didn't take long to become disheartened at the idea that most likely I'd never birth out of me who or even what God had purposed for my life before my formation.

At a young age, I had an extreme awareness of God's presence flowing through my veins, but at that time, I wasn't exactly sure, nor did I understand how to connect with him. What I understood more than anything was my life was subtly being molded, but into what was the question. The very individuals God had given charge over my life along with his mandate to help me experience and examine the world through a different set of eyes would ultimately become the same individuals who would impart in me all their weaknesses, insecurities, and fears.

14

The many unhealthy gravel roads I'd end up traveling down during my journey to adulthood would be directed by fear. Seamlessly incorporating itself into my daily life, it didn't take fear long before introducing its many different personalities. Abandonment was one of the first personalities who entered quite abruptly. Shaking hands, abandonment and I met when I started preschool. For me, abandonment was feminine in nature because she was very much linked to my mother.

At the close of each school day, I'd watch the ecstatic faces of my preschool classmates light up as parents walked through our classroom door. One by one, they would shuffle in, gather up the day's activities and with child-in-hand, quickly disappear. Once the last of my classmates were gone, abandonment, which had been lurking in some dark corner, would crawl out of its place of solace to keep me company. The nature in how she worked in my life became recognizable, and I would always know when she was there. She'd embrace me with deception, whispering lies that I'd never see my mother again, and it was my mother who had actually sent her to be a comfort to me.

Why my life had been so important to abandonment at such a young age remains a mystery. At four years old, I knew her very intimately, and she knew me. Maybe there had been a door left slightly cracked throughout the generations, and fear along with its many personalities had been stealth in their ability to slither through. Abandonment was only one of the fragmented identities of fear. I ultimately would encounter others. The only question was when they would enter my life, introducing themselves.

As I got older, I met abuse, and she came in like a whirlwind. She was definitely very different than abandonment because she had been granted the power and ability to display herself mentally, emotionally, and at full maturity, physically in my life. I could tell her force was much more powerful. Abuse's presence demanded attention and was explicit in the ways she chose to be seen and heard. She was never alone when she made her appearance. With her came an accomplice whose name was manipulation. Manipulation would rear its head only when necessary and when employed upon. I didn't quite understand all the details of their relationship, but I saw that manipulation and abuse somehow fit like a hand in glove.

Both would show up whenever my mother needed to remind my siblings and myself that she was in control over our lives. As she worked on my hair one afternoon, she adamantly let me know if I didn't participate in a fashion show alongside the teens of her coworkers, I could look forward to her no longer providing for my needs. This was not an isolated incident. Just one of many. I felt very broken, knowing she needed me to be more like the children of her friends, who were military wives. For some reason, they were better, and for my mom, me simply being me wasn't good enough for her. I somehow needed to be more. I somehow needed to be better. I needed to be everything else other than the daughter she had carried and given birth to. That person had never been good enough. It was mostly my mother who would continuously thrust me into the arms of fear and all its cohorts, whether done consciously or subconsciously. She helped define how fear manifested in my life. Without safeguards in place and no protection from the terrors of the world, I spent a large measure of my journey searching out resuscitation for my soul. Unfortunately, I did this without any knowledge of where to start. I had no idea what I was searching for, what it looked, felt, or even sounded like. Without any guidance, ultimately, I'd end up walking through many wrong doors, and without the slightest hesitancy, they had so graciously opened wide, inviting me to come inside.

Where was God? I was in this long and obscure war that seemingly had no end, and many of the wounds from it I'd carry well into adulthood. Internally, I felt wounded and slowly dying on side of the road as people observed while passing me by from the other side. My mother had become an individual whom I no longer recognized, yet I still desperately needed the woman who would pick me up as a child, placing me on her hip. God's silence was deafening, and I had to feel my way through the puzzling darkness without answers.

It was painful knowing I had only been a disappointment in my mother's life. Her words, which pierced and wounded, reiterated that disappointment. I can only guess that she needed to constantly remind me because of who she needed me to be and who I was becoming were total opposites. I often wonder when the exact moment in time occurred where she had designed within herself the image of what the perfect daughter entailed. I had longed abandoned that image for my life because I knew I could never measure up to it. What I needed more than anything was understanding my path and what my overall journey was about. I knew my mother would not be the one to help me understand that path nor strengthen me through the journey. I was alone.

Acceptance finally entered my life when I understood the only person I could change was the person who stared back from the mirror. God's imprint slowly unraveled as I continued developing into my own person. My mom had only been an instrument in his overall plan. In my forties, I made a deliberate decision to forgive her, which brought an indescribable freedom.

All the burdens and bitterness could no longer continue to sink their nails into my soul. Smiling, I knew she somehow felt it also although I'd never be able to express and deliver the words to her that my spirit was speaking. I knew God would. He would be the one delivering the news that I'd let go of the pain I'd held tightly to since childhood. I was not just a survivor, but more than anything, I was an overcomer because of the power of choice.

Choice and the power it held reigned mightily in my life. I couldn't pinpoint the exact moment where I felt it penetrate, but it was more like a line in a movie I saw once—one day you wake up and decide to not be mad anymore. My suddenly had simply overtaken me although I didn't realize it was happening. I had to purposely choose to not allow fear and its many faces to continue directing my life as it pleased. This was what brought freedom and placed me on a different journey. It is the message I will share with others who have gone before me and those who will also follow. Releasing the pain my mother had imparted through who she was placed my life on a new course.

I finally started winning by making a purposed decision to understand who God had created when I was only a simple thought to him. If no one else chose me, I knew God had chosen me from the beginning. Winning starts with grabbing ahold of the power we have within that he has given to each of us, only if we will choose it. Release those we've held in bondage for years and embrace the healing that awaits us. This is what takes our lives down a different path. Our effectiveness is in understanding we have others who quietly wait for us to rise from of the ashes because they are connected to our lives. They need to hear our voices and witness our victories.

Say yes to a simple decision of releasing all fears, disappointments, pains, and unforgiveness. Step into purpose through the power that choice presents. Understand and know you were designed for it even if you don't recognize it. Know that it's there inside you. Nothing and no one in this life can stop your journey except you. There's victory in purposely choosing to win.

A Blessed Mess

Tanya A. Roquemore

Remember how the story of Cinderella began with "Once upon a time…" and there was a happy ending? It seemed like life was so simple then, and everything was easy. It really was easier because we believed that life would end up being just like that fairy tale, and we would grow up and find our Prince Charming. He was handsome, rich, and had a house on the hill. Everyone wanted to be the princess, and we never really worried about what happened in between. *Then, we grew up.*

For me, I wasn't the fairy tale kind of girl. I was the dreamer. I spent days and days dreaming of my perfect wedding…the bridesmaids all dressed in baby blue with bonnets (yes, bonnets with long sheer ribbons down the back). The men in black tux, and that FINE MAN standing at the altar in a white tux, big and strong, he was going to be my husband. He had to be large in stature because as I became his wife, I was foolish enough to believe that he was created by God to be my protector. *He was my dream.*

I longed for the dates, the walks, the conversations. I knew that just like on *Leave It to Beaver*, we would have children, and every problem in the world would be resolved in thirty minutes. They never encountered crime, drugs, or molestation. The last thing that would ever happen is domestic violence because things don't happen like that on TV, and it would never happen in my dream marriage either. *Then, I grew up.*

The reality of being born and raised in South Central Los Angeles was a harsh awakening to the cruel world that would come to exist. But that didn't bother me much because my parents were wise enough to send me to private school where I would receive a wonderful education. My daddy told me that I was beautiful and smart. I had talent, charisma, and the ability to talk to anybody about anything.

My mother owned a beauty salon, and her customers would say I had an old soul. Mr. Pops, the local numbers runner, would always say, "That girl been here before." Mommy said I told him, "I have been here before, but I didn't see you!" That smart mouth of mine would eventually lead me to a lot of trouble, but for the time, it was cute. I believed that I would not only conquer the world, but I would also run it. I would grow up to be Ms. America and President of the United States. *I was 5.*

The calling of the streets was loud, and the voices would not be silenced. I fell in love with the roar, and my father raised me to understand that his baby girl possessed all the tools that I would ever need to get anything that I ever desired. With time, I became aware of street life, and the dreams of Ms. America began to fade as children would tease me because my hair was short, and my skin was discolored and rough due to eczema.

Because of this harassment, I stopped believing that I was beautiful and learned that I was ugly. For the first time in my life, I discovered that my parents LIED! I resented them for allowing me to believe in ME. I faulted them because what my parents meant for my good led to isolation, depression, and even suicidal thoughts. Yes, this was my childhood, privileged with material blessings and a great educational environment and a yet internally deprived of the joy every child deserves. *I was 12.*

I slept in the bed of pity many nights and greeted the morning struggle with a smile because that was what I was taught. Please note that my belief system was very different from my learned behavior. So, I smiled through it all, be strong girl, never let them see you shed a tear. Do whatever it takes to get the attention you desire. Even if that attention came from the neighborhood bookie I called Uncle Tim. He was the one that demonstrated what it meant to be a woman and be able to get whatever you desire.

It was a Monday afternoon, I had just come home from school, and Mommy told me to go downstairs and put clothes in the washer. I didn't feel like it, and so of course that smart mouth went to work on Mommy. She got her way, and I found myself downstairs doing laundry, and Uncle Tim came down to talk to me and explain that I was not supposed to talk to my mother like that. "Ok, and!"

Uncle Tim was smooth, handsome, salt and pepper beard, and the man smelled like a mixture of manly cologne and cigarettes. Hindsight, that was horrible, but at the time, it wasn't bad, and he was giving me attention. He hugged me, told me I was too beautiful to act like that. I believed him. The he touched my chest. I didn't know it at the time, but I was developed. He told me that as long as I had these, I didn't have to act like that, and I could have anything I wanted. *I believed him.*

With that confidence from Uncle Tim, I went back upstairs and talked with my mom. Uncle Tim eventually left, and I told my mommy what he told me, and most importantly, what he did. I had never seen my mom so angry, hurt, and it was the first time the .38 Smith and Wesson came out in the middle of the day. She called him with a few choice words, and I never saw Uncle Tim again. *I was still 12.*

The struggle was difficult as low self-esteem became my best friend, and it led me down a path filled with abuse, homosexuality, being bullied, and drugs. Like so many others with a repertoire full of tragic episodes, I became a victim. Uncle Tim was the first to touch me, and it seemed he set the pace for what became a pattern for my young life. The same year, during a trip to Vegas with my mom, a stranger found me in the game room at a casino while my mom was playing her slot machine, and I was playing video games. He touched me then followed us around Vegas waiting for my mom to leave me again. I thought I might have found a boyfriend to give me attention. Not the case.

I was a child wanting attention, needing to be told that I was beautiful and that I had value. I wanted to know that I could be attractive because remember the kids told me I was ugly, and I believed them. It continued, the boys in the closet, the kids playing on the street, my cousin's friends, the man at the bicycle shop...it just never seemed to stop.

A pivotal point when my innocence was totally shattered was the summer of my freshman year of high school. Mommy wanted to make sure I was never late, so she put me on the bus early. There was the coolest guy on the bus every morning, and he stared at me all the time. I KNEW he liked me, so the morning he got off the bus and walked me the three blocks to school I was excited! He didn't like me. He raped me.

I told Col Hughes, the principal, most of the story, but of course was too embarrassed to ever tell anyone what really happened, how I was dragged to the alley behind the apartments. He called my mother and advised her not to send me to school so early.

I say this was pivotal because it was the very moment that I never wanted to be touched by a man again. They HURT! I was damaged. I was worthless. I was UGLY.

My entire life changed, and I discovered that women love differently.

I was 41 years old, and it was about a year before my mother transitioned; she questioned what happened to her baby girl who dreamed of the beautiful wedding, strong handsome husband, and house full of kids. I believe she knew something happened when she asked, "Were you raped?"

"Yes, Mommy, I was."

We understood what was unspoken.

But with that single question, my life began to change again. I realized that I spent too many years living in the comfort of a victim's fears. My heart had not smiled, and as a stud, I portrayed the character of the person I longed to be loved by, never allowing anyone to know me, touch me, or love me. I wasn't the person that I had become. I became the person I hated and feared.

The victory happened the day I woke up and realized that I was not purposed for tragedy but for triumph. I discovered that, while lying in the gutter of emotional defeat, I would smile again. That 5-year-old girl was still inside willing to thrive; SHE had survived. It is in that very moment of being slain that I became the slayer. I got up, I slayed my fears, I slayed the physical abuse, I slayed low self-esteem. I became; therefore, I am.

I still hear my daddy's voice saying, "Remember that as a woman you can have anything that you desire." Three things I learned that every woman should know and believe are **#1:** YOU ARE AN OVERCOMMER, **#2:** YOUR PAST IS NOT YOUR TRASH; IT IS YOUR TREASURE, and **#3:** YOU ARE FEARFULLY AND WONDERFULLY MADE.

Today, I am 54. It took a while, but I began to dream again. I believe again. I trust again.

Girl, Get Up and Win…you are truly a BLESSED MESS.

I Want My Daddy

Shearese Stapleton

"Shearese, make sure you have clean underwear and three sets of clothes," my mother shouted upstairs.

You see, it was the weekend, and it was time to go be with my dad, and my 10-year-old self was getting ready. I couldn't find my other shoe.

"Mom, do see my red gym shoe down there?" I asked.

"No. That is why I tell you to put them on your steps."

I sat by the bed and began to cry, then said to myself, "Shearese, why do you always lose stuff? Daddy will be here, and he is going to be upset if he has to wait on you. You always do this. What is wrong with you?"

I cried as I crawled on the floor, looking under the bed and in my closet. My mother came upstairs and found me frantically looking for my shoe. Still crying, I said, "I always do this when he is on his way, Momma. I'm sorry. I may just have to wear the old ones, or I will just ask him to buy a new pair. Yeah, Momma, I'll just ask Daddy to buy me a new pair."

I looked at Momma, and she had a look on her face. "What's wrong, Momma?" I asked. "I will find the shoe when I get back. I know it's here somewhere."

My mother stopped me from looking for the shoe and pulled me up to sit on the bed.

"What's wrong, Momma? Why are you sad, Momma?"

"Shearese," she finally spoke, "he is not coming!"

"What? I just talked to him, Momma. He said he was coming when he got from the store."

Momma looked at me and said, "Baby, he is not coming!"

This was what would happen at least three to four times out of every other weekend visit I would have with my dad, and you would think by now I would be used to it, but no, I was a 10-year-old little girl who adored her dad and loved him so much, and every time he was supposed to come, I was ready!

My mother and father were high school sweethearts, and they were such a cute couple from what I have been told. My mom has always been short, so in their prom picture, her head came to my dad's chest. My grandmother told me the story of how my mom and dad were in love and how much they wanted to have a baby, so that's what they did. But they were 15 and 16, so I'm going to say they might not had known what love really was. Nevertheless, I was born August 28, 1973, at 10:00 a.m. at Hurly Medical Center in Flint, Michigan, weighing a whopping two pounds three ounces…and two months early.

27

Even though my parents were in love, they fought a lot—I mean a whole lot. It was to the point my grandfather forbade my dad to come to my mom's house. And the night before I was born, my mom and dad got into a really big fight, and that is what made me come early.

When you are a little girl, the way you view your dad is the way you begin to view all men.

From that point on, my relationships were designed to fail within a two- to six-month time span, and if they ended beforehand, they were not to be. Worse than that, if the relationship seemed too good to be true, I would sabotage it somehow. I felt like I should mess up the relationships before I let the person hurt me, not knowing I was predicting the future. This was from abandonment issues.

I learned that back when my dad was calling my mom and telling her that he could not come, he was putting women before me. Just so happened that as my mom and I were going to the store, we past him in the car, and he was with a woman—when he was supposed to pick me up. It felt like that scene from *The Fresh Prince of Bel Air* when Will, devastated over his father's lack of care, asked his uncle, "How come he don't want me, man?"

In my middle school years, I was not getting along with one person in my mom's house: my stepfather. It wasn't his fault. I became very angry because my dad was not married to my mom, and I just could not understand why my sister got to have her daddy. I understand now why I was such an angry middle school child.

During my middles school years, my mom had a conversation with my dad and my grandmother (my dad's mom) for me to go live with them for a while. This was how I got to learn about how my dad had those same bouts of anger that I did. It was like when his emotions would overtake him, he would holler or leave the house. My grandmother had a way with him that would calm him down, and he would listen to her. When I became a teenager, I had that same way my grandmother had with my dad. I could talk him down out of his anger.

In 1991, I graduated from high school, and it was the best moment of my life up until that point.

I had always been short, so I had the lady who fit me for my gown to add an inch to the length because I knew I would be wearing heels that day, and I knew that I would feel as though I was ten feet tall. I stepped on the stage of N-Dub at five foot three instead of five foot two with white heels, hair curled, and ready to be independent and grown into what I believe a women should be. That was just one of the ways my family was known for dressing. My whole family was there from my mother's side to my dad's side; it was one of the most meaningful days of my life. My dad was so proud of me. I was a second generation graduate from high school. I almost didn't make it to that stage. If it wasn't for my grandmother who said, "Shearese, if you go to school every day, I will let you drive my car," I might not have graduated. It was the first time that I was given responsibility for my life.

Now, to make all of this make sense—I'm now the mother of three wonderful, amazing people who went through a time of their mother being angry and not truly understanding why, and nothing but God could change it. You see, when you witness anger due to not being able to change or control someone, you either grow up exemplifying those same signs or you suppress it, and then it comes out looking like depression, or you not being satisfied, and even you expecting someone to make you happy. Now what I need you to know is that no one is responsible for your happiness but you. Most of us women are looking for a husband, children, education, career, and even marital things to make us happy! My relationship with my father as a child shaped how I viewed men. I understand it now; I was always looking for a replacement to be the daddy. My friends had the daddies who were calm and present in their lives.

My name is Shearese, and my father loves me, but that relationship does not define who I am today. For every woman who is responsible for the little girl who was not picked up on time by her father, I pray that you allow God to strengthen your emotional heath. That you love your daughter unconditionally and forever remind her that his actions have nothing to do with her. What I want you to get from this chapter in my life is to understand you are responsible for your own happiness. Other people can assist in what that looks like, but when it's all said and done, it's up to you.

The little girl has now grown up to be a lady who knows who she wants to become. This happened one day when I asked God to show me how to not be angry and how to love me better than anyone ever could. And it happened—with help from research and time and study.

In the summer of 2019, I will launch a girls leadership program called Successful Girl Boss Leadership. This program is designed to strengthen the leadership in girls from middle school to high school and put them in the place of understanding self-love.

I am also founder and CEO of Mothers of Joy University where empowering families is a way of life. The organization provides parents with opportunities to learn alongside their children and also to have meaningful conversations. Our lifelong slogan is "Come Let's Learn Together."

Thank you for taking time to hear my truth and how I started a journey of understanding that has given me a true and new outlook on life!

What I Didn't Have a Father/Daddy to Teach Me

Sharee Williams

Father: A present male, brings life into the world, participates, loves, to place responsibility on.

Notice the definition of a father; anyone can be a father by name, but it takes a special type of male to display the attributes and qualities of a true father. I was born in a two-parent home, but by life's circumstances, my father passed early in my life, leaving me to not have the opportunity to experience being daddy's little girl and experience the things that little girls love to experience with having a father. Things like father-daughter dances, learning how to ride a bike, pulling my first tooth, going on a first date, having a man open and hold doors for me, and seeing how a man should treat me as woman.

Ok, so let's go back a bit—after the passing of my father. I ended up in foster care until the age of nine or ten years old, at which time I was returned home to my mother and having to find my true identity in a whole new environment and with a family I no longer recognized and with much different values than what I had been used to for the past nine or ten years. This means I had to grow up faster than the average child whose father had been present. My mom was great in raising me, but she could not teach me how a man should treat me. She did, however, teach me how she wanted a man to treat her and how she thought a man should be treated, which had qualities that she only knew—qualities that were based on stereotypical male bashing jargon. Things such as all men are dogs, they only want one thing, they don't want anything beyond the physical, and you do whatever it takes to keep a roof over your head and your bills paid. Even when you get married, you are nothing more than a piece of meat to a man, that it is your job as a woman to make sure that your man feels like a king even when you are feeling less than worthy and unhappy.

I did not have a father to correct any of the destructive behavior and misconceptions of what a father/daddy should resemble. My daddy was not able tell me you don't have to sleep with every male to get your bills paid and to get your needs met; my daddy was not able to teach me that not all men are dogs; my daddy was not able to teach me that is was not my job to be strong and independent (let's not take this line out of context because it does have its place); my daddy wasn't there to show me what the role of a father should be in a family setting; my daddy was not there to show me what was acceptable when a man asked me out on a date; and my daddy was not able to show me what a real man should be.

Needless to say, at seventeen, I began dating without any concept of what qualities I should be looking for in a man, leaving me to get inadequate affections and behaviors in my relationships. As I began dating and having children, I got into relationships that had no substance; in other words, I was dating without a purpose. These "boys" had no respect for me; they were physically, emotionally, and verbally abusive, and I had no clue that this was wrong, that this was not how I should be treated. I was supposed to be looking for a father for my children, not just having babies by random "boys" and raising them alone. How is a young girl supposed to know that without the proper guidance? With the mindset that no matter what, these are my babies, and I got this and will make it work even if that means doing it alone. Don't misunderstand me. I did date them, but they had no good qualities, no substance about them, but when you are young, you think you have it all figured out. Looking back after my fourth child, I realized they did not. You may ask, Sharee, how did you realize that, and why did it take you so long to realize that the men you were dating had no qualities? Well, up until my fifth child, I did just what Mama said to do—make and keep that man happy by any means necessary. I did whatever a man wanted to me do. If he cheated, I pretended I didn't know about it. If he did not want to give money unless I was giving him something in return, I did what he wanted me do. If he wanted me not to have no life, I did not have a life. After all, my mom was right as far as I knew. I had no one to tell me or show me anything different.

After the separating from my fourth child's father, I was left with just me and my children, and I thought, I don't think this is how it's supposed to be. I became very bitter toward men, and I had a wall up.

I promised myself that I was not going to allow myself to get into another situation like that, honestly how can you not? After being single and a mother of five children for the past three years, I met the man that would soon become my husband. I thought my life was falling to pieces because here was a man that was the opposite of what I was taught a man should be, a man that would share in doing everything as a partner. Everything Momma told me I had to do to keep a man, like cook and clean, my future husband really did without expecting anything in return. A man that would love not one but five other children that were not his. Wow, I was blown away because a man was willing to stay while I fought through my own insecurities and imperfections and the toxicity I brought into the relationship. I would do any and everything to destroy this relationship because it wasn't toxic. Although that's not the icing on the cake, the icing was when we had our first child (he wasn't my husband yet). He didn't leave; he stayed and said he wasn't going anywhere. I was not ready for this because every other mate I had left me to raise my children on my own. I did not know how to deal with this because my daddy was not there to teach me that these were traits and qualities of a man. I called everyone I knew and asked them, "Why is he still here?"

"Isn't he supposed to leave?"

That's when I realized that I had daddy issues because not having a daddy, I did not know how to allow a real man to love and treat me or honestly, I didn't know how to treat myself. The anger from being mistreated by men and the wall I had built up toward men carried into other areas of my life, such as making sound decisions, advancing in careers, and maintaining friendships and other relationships in general. I had to learn that everything a man had done to me was because I had allowed it. My misconception of men was formed by generational issues. You see, my mother's father was not in her life, my grandmother's father was not in her life, so how could she honestly tell what a good man is, and what a good father truly should be? She couldn't, and when I realize that, it was an eye opener for me, and it was not pretty at all. I had to go beyond the superficial part of me, meaning I had to go past blaming my mom, not taking responsibilities for my part in this dysfunction and dig down deep to that ugliness, that part of me that I did not want to see and did not want anyone else to see to the root of why I couldn't keep a job, to why I could not maintain not just friendships but good healthy relationships, and come to the realization that nope my daddy could not teach me the things that I needed to know about men, but if I truly wanted to know what a good man was I would have to go outside of my circle and my finite mind to see examples of good men and not just be limited to what was in my comfort zone, a place that allowed me to settle for less than what I deserved in every area of my life. And now that I have broadened my horizons and understand that I had these daddy issues because my daddy wasn't present and able teach me, I can now be a better me.

When We Say "I do"

Overcoming the Greatest Enemy Within to Win!

Dr. Sakeisha and Eric Hylick

Have you ever found yourself running at full speed on ALL cylinders? Chasing or in pursuit of what you thought was success? In the midst of that, you find yourself forgetting why you were running? I mean there has got to be more to life than finding that special someone, getting married, paying bills, raising kids, getting a house and a car and perhaps some grandiose title, right? Somehow in the midst of all of that, you still felt empty on the inside. If we can be totally transparent with you, we found ourselves at this point. It was during this phase we had every material thing imaginable, but our relationship was in trouble. Seriously, we:

- Drove the nicest cars
- Built our dream home (at the time)
- Had our kids enrolled in the best private schools

- Had a marriage that from the outside looking in everyone wanted
- Went to church regularly and were in positions of leaderships

Yet with all these things, we felt that we had nothing at the same time, if that makes sense. We live in an age where people are constantly evaluating you based on:

- Your social media profile
- The number of likes
- How many followers you have
- How packed out your conferences are, etc.

Being in a state of constantly comparing your life, your business, and especially your relationships can truly eat away at the very fibers of your being if you aren't secure in who you are and who you are called to be.

We did not want to spend the next 10 years chasing after money, only to be back at the same place: emotionally, mentally, physically, and spiritually bankrupt. We realized that if our relationship was going to **WIN**, if we were not going to follow in our parents' footsteps with marriage after marriage failing, we had to do something drastically different! We had to put pride aside. We had spent so much time pouring into others and trying to be who others thought that we should be that we lost sight of who we truly were and began to drift apart. We had to put in some serious time and develop the mindset of a winner. Successful relationships do not just happen; if our **Only Option was going to be to WIN**, we had to shift our mindset in order to **Overcome the Enemy Within**.

Now you may be saying to yourself, this sounds good, but what did the two of you do to go from where you were back then to where you now? We realized that we had to overcome the underlying issues that were swept under the rug that when allowed to manifest began to hold us back. All of that hard work began to tear at the fiber of our marriage until the point that we were no longer husband and wife but had become roommates.

We incorporated **3 Key Strategies to Overcome the Enemy Within so that We Could Win.**

Point #1: Take a Look in the Mirror

Do you like what you see? Not just the physical aspect, but look deeper. We had to learn to embrace not only our physical imperfections but the emotional and mental aspects of it.

- When was the last time you seriously took ownership of the role that you contributed to your relationship?
- Have you ever considered how much time you are actually spending trying to please people?

I mean really, to be honest with yourselves. If we can be completely transparent, people pleasing was wearing us out. We were drained physically, emotionally, financially, and spiritually. When you find yourself at a point where you pour out so much unto others that you do not have enough time for your spouse, when your spouse is getting what is left over, it's time to change that quickly. We had to intentionally schedule regular time together. We either had to make our marriage a priority, or divorce was going to be our reality. So choose wisely. Whether it's a weekly date night or a trip or staycation, successful partners are intentional with their time to make sure that they connect with one another regularly.

Take the next 5-10 minutes and jot down the amount of time you are willing to dedicate to helping your relationship/marriage grow. For example, every Friday after 5 p.m., I commit to shutting off my phone and giving my spouse my undivided attention, then schedule what the two of us are going to commit to do on those evenings. If you are going to dinner, go bowling, take a walk in the park, etc., schedule the baby sitter if you need one and make it happen.

_____

_____

_____

_____

_____

_____

_____

_____

_____

Point #2: Learn the Power of the Word NO!

The two simple letters literally saved our marriage! If you take out your smartphone or planner and look at your schedule:

- Is your spouse a priority on there?
- How many other things take priority over them?
- How many dinners have been cancelled or forgotten because the two of you were "too busy"?

While it is great to be a generous, supportive friend, confidant, business professional, it can be a double-edged sword. It's remarkable how people will ask of you at times attempt to demand your time, your attention, and or your finances. It is imperative that you protect yourself and your relationship by being bold enough to say these two letters: NO.

No further explanation required! It is extremely easy to lose sight of your own relationship when you are focusing on helping someone else accomplish their goals. We get it, you're a good person with a great heart; however,

- No is a powerful tool to have in your relationship survival skills toolkit;
- No demonstrates to your spouse that the time you have together is valuable and should not be taken for granted;
- No teaches others to respect you and your time; and

- No helps you to delineate between your personal life and your professional life.

When did we come to this realization?
The last time that I passed out at my job and paramedics had to pick me up off the floor while my patients were looking at me in disbelief. In their minds, I was Superwoman. After all, I was their go-to person. They believed that I could handle all of their insurance problems, contact all of their doctors, counsel them on their medications, handle the department scheduling, coach other healthcare professionals that had questions about how to handle different scenarios, assist with training staff, and resolve conflict all in under 15 minutes or less. Seeing the sheer panic on my husband's face as he rushed to meet me before the ambulance whisked me away to the hospital helped us to put things in proper perspective. Not to mention the amount of money that I had to invest in a therapist to help me deal with the need that I had to be the best at everything. For the second time, I had allowed my job to heap additional responsibilities upon me that were stealing my time from what was really important to me. My husband and my children were receiving what was left over, if anything, after I left work. Our sex life was virtually non-existent, and I was grouchy, easily agitated, and NEVER satisfied. This was not fair to them, so we decided that it was time to take back control over our lives and start using those two simple letters NO to help.

What are two to three things that you could start saying no to that will help you Overcome the Enemy Within so That Winning Is Your Only Option?

_____

_____

_____

_____

_____

_____

_____

_____

Point # 3 Express What You Expect

Couples these days are often struggling with:

- Balancing successful careers
- Being entrepreneurs
- Managing families
- Maintaining Successful relationships

We know that time is a precious commodity that one can ill afford to waste by holding onto grudges. Your spouse is NOT a mind reader. Remember, the two of you are in this relationship together; therefore, it is going to require effort from both of you in order for your relationship to succeed. Successful couples recognize that expressing their needs sooner versus later helps them avoid the buildup and eruption of emotions. Can I remind you that he/she cannot meet a need that they do not know exists? Like many couples, this was a bitter pill for us to swallow. Our assumption was that we had been together for so long that we expected one another to just know what to do, or what to say, or how to respond. Really? We had to invest the time to get know what our partner's needs are.

- What are their **sexual needs**?
- What are their **emotional needs**?
- What are their **financial needs**?

Don't assume. As we get older, our needs change, and we need to keep having these open dialogues so we are equipped to handle them. Let's be real, the person you are at this phase in your life is drastically different from who you were 5 years ago, 10 years, heck even 1 year ago. For all of you business owners, career execs, times are changing. You can't run your business the same now on the same technology that you did two to three years ago. You have to invest the time necessary to address those changes, so our question to you is, *When was the last time that the two of you did a* **Relationship Checkup**?

Find out the following:

- What does your partner want from you now that they are not receiving?
- How have their needs changed?

- What you can do to help?

Today, we tend to avoid conflict, so we are walking around with unmet needs, frustrated, aggravated, and about to explode. When people walk in fear and are afraid to express what their expectations are, what tends to happen is people harness their disappointments and walk away from relationships that can be salvaged, not knowing that each person comes with their own set of baggage. This carries on from one relationship to the next until these needs are ultimately expressed and addressed.

Set yourselves up so that Winning Is Your Only Option by **1) Taking a Look in the Mirror, 2) Learning the Power of the Word No, and 3) Expressing What You Expect.**

The Binding Tie

Terra Kern

As I lay in my bed crying over my husband being out drinking with the boys again, I looked over at the clock and saw it glowing the time as two o'clock in the morning. My heart felt as though it were breaking in two. I was at my wit's end. This is not the marriage I had anticipated or the way I wanted my 2-month-old daughter to be raised.

I took in another deep breath, and as I let it out, I began to cry out to God, whom I had not followed for the past few years due to the folly of my youth. As I prayed, all of the troubles of my heart began to pour out. The floodgates had been opened.

"Dear God, please help me. He's out drinking again, and I can't take it anymore! I don't know what to do. The divorce papers Daddy had drawn up by his attorney are just waiting for my signature. I don't want to sign them. I don't want to sin against you, but I don't want to live with an alcoholic for a husband, and I don't want the precious baby girl you gave me to grow up with a father addicted to alcohol either. I thought his drinking was a young man thing, and when he became a father, he would grow up, give it up, and become a responsible man. That hasn't happened.

"I have made such a mess of my life, and worse yet, I now have a new little life that I am responsible for, too. Please come and live within me again and lead me in the way to go. I tried living my life on my own and have made a huge disaster of it. I need you in my life again. Lead me and guide me in the way to go by your Holy Spirit, I pray."

Suddenly, I felt as light as a feather, as though I were levitating. I was sure when I opened my eyes I would be a mere few inches from the ceiling. But when I opened them, I was still lying in my bed and not floating at all. I felt a peaceful calm come over me as I looked to my right and saw a faint light in the shape of a long robe with outstretched arms and distinct hands reaching out to me. I heard a voice in the room audibly and gently say to me, "Fear not, my little child, for I will take care of things."

The next thing I knew, I was awoken by the sound of my husband stumbling through the house and falling onto the couch in the living room. I found myself thanking God that he had made it home safely and rolled over to go back to sleep. This was a new thing for me because I normally would have gotten out of bed and tore into him, yapping and nipping like a high strung poodle, letting him know exactly what I thought of him and his drinking. But not this time, for I was encompassed by a sweet peace.

Sunday rolled around, and my parents stopped by on their way to church and asked if I wanted to go. I literally felt something inside of me leap for joy! And for the first time, I told them I wanted to go rather than making my tired and worn out excuses.

Every Sunday, they invited me, and I went. Every Sunday, I invited my husband, and he declined. Every Sunday, God was moving in the church, and testimonies were shared on the wonderful things God had blessed people with in their lives. Every Sunday, Pastor prayed for people, and God moved. And every Sunday, I came home and shared these things with my husband.

One Sunday shortly thereafter, I was in the living room dressed for church when out of the blue, my husband walked into the living room dressed in his good clothes and informed me he wanted to go to church and see about the things I had been telling him. I was so surprised and even more happy!

After the sermon, Pastor instructed the organist to play as he prayed. He silently bowed his head and, after a few moments, made an announcement. He shared with the congregation that there was someone who God was calling and asked everyone to bow their heads, close their eyes, and pray silently. Pastor invited whomever God was speaking to, to come forward. There was nothing but organ music quietly playing, but no movement.

I knew God was calling my husband, so I gently reached over and touched his hand. I whispered if he wanted me to go up with him, I would. He promptly put my hand back on my lap and whispered to me, "If I'm going up there, it will be because I want to, not because someone else wants me to."

I was shocked and hurt, but continued to pray. The church was silent except for the organist playing. Pastor called for that person once more, and to my glee, my husband stood up, walked to the altar, and dedicated his life to God! That was the day God intervened, kept His promise to me, and saved our marriage!

Our lives and marriage were transformed. My husband gave up alcohol on the spot. He hungered for the things of God, and we were in church every time the doors were open. He began to serve our pastor in many capacities, from hard labor to ushering. We eventually became head deacons, counseling young married couples while we served as part of the ministerial staff.

Ladies, when you put God in the center of your marriage, a threefold cord is created with Him being the binding tie. And as Scripture says, a threefold cord is not easily broken! Our marriage had struggles as every marriage does, but with each struggle overcome through prayer and scripture, it grew stronger. As a result, my husband and I are in our 36th year of marriage and have three wonderful children and eight delightful grandchildren.

Let's Stay Together

Dr. Ladel Lewis

Let's, let's stay together (gether)
Lovin' you whether, whether
Times are good or bad, happy or sad

Al Green, "Let's Stay Together" (1972)

Marriage is a beautiful thing. Two souls becoming one in holy matrimony. A selfless act that many never get the privilege to experience. Unfortunately, a countless number of people go an entire lifetime without an official life partner. They may have someone they engage in casual sex with for an extended time (also referred to as "messing around") or perhaps even someone they cohabitate with (affectionately known as "shacking up"). Neither of which require the level of immediate commitment necessary in marriage. Some people experience several failed attempts at this thing called "love" and become discouraged to the point of losing hope. Is that grounds to give up on it? Absolutely not. It's grounds to keep going. It's grounds to keep on fighting for this coveted feeling that we all seek, this strong affection from another.

While this is the warm and fuzzy side of a relationship, let's face it, when you meet your life partner, everything may appear to be great on the surface because we are in "sales mode." We are on our best behavior and putting our best foot forward in an effort to impress. The second you are "locked-in" and all of the walls come down, the representative is pink-slipped, and the real person reports for duty. The newness has worn off.

When this happens, are you going to throw the baby away with the bathwater? Not so fast. If you meant what you said when you stood before the judge or the preacher, you want to work through it all. In the words of the great Reverend Al Green, you want to "stay together." Who gets married to get divorced? Who spends money on rings, wedding planners, venues, wardrobe, photographers, and the like just to watch their investment go up in smoke? In the words of my mother, "Oh, hell no!" Unless your family is wealthy, and you have unlimited years to put toward a fruitless relationship, that is not an option. Those of us who are not so fortunate are in it to win it unless extenuating circumstances beg to differ. Uttering the words, "For better and for worse, for richer, for poorer, in sickness and in health, to love and cherish always" means that we are in it for the long haul. It is in no way easy but is definitely doable and worth it. Here are four steps to help you retain your sanity while attempting to keep it together.

Step One: Honest Communication

What I need from you is understanding
How can we communicate
If you don't hear what I say

Xscape, "Understanding" (1993)

Have you ever seen a couple out to dinner sitting in complete silence? They sit there as if they are eating alone all the while checking their social media accounts or playing games on their cell phones. I've seen this too many times, and I have wondered, "Wow, why come out for dinner if you're not going speak with your companion?" I've never done this because I always have so much to say. Being able to keep a conversation going is one of my strong points. That is why I thought my fiancé and I were doing great in this area. We used to talk about the latest happenings in the media, our day, and the latest family news. I thought we were communicating effectively. To my surprise, we were not. We were not "dating." I learned that dating or going out on a date means collecting data on the other person. You need to know important information about them. What is their attitude about children, money, and their parents? Do they want children? If so, what is their parenting style? Are you the only one desiring a suburban life with a family of four with a picket fence and a dog? If so, their idea of living in a condo in the heart of a big city may not align with your goals. This thorough vetting will help you determine if they are really ready to pursue or maintain holy matrimony with you, or if they need to level up. Financially speaking, you also need to discuss your income, assets, debts, and liabilities. In Laymen's terms, how much money do you bring in, how much do you owe, and what does your credit score look like? You can't do anything without credit. You can't make major purchases, buy insurance, or even rent a home in many cases. Their credit score tells a lot about their attitude toward money. That is why your credit reports and scores should be a topic of discussion if you are serious about securing a future with one another. What you don't know WILL hurt you.

Step Two: Don't Be Nag-a-licious

Spending all my time pleasing you
All you ever give me is the blues

Tony! Toni! Toné!, "The Blues" (1990)

Do you tend to want to do your best when someone is nagging you? No? It doesn't make you want to put that extra pep in your step and go over and beyond the call of duty? Well, your mate is no different. That's exactly how your mate feels when you nag them. Instead of making them want to change, it makes them want to do the exact opposite. For the extreme naggers, it may make them want to run to the arms of someone less burdensome.

At the beginning of my marriage, I fell into this trap. For example, back home, we call cleaning the entire kitchen "washing dishes," and I *wash dishes* a particular way. After I wash the dishes in the sink, I wipe down all of the countertops, thoroughly clean the stove, and sweep the kitchen floor. When hubby cleans the kitchen, he leaves a puddle of water on the counter, does not sweep the floor, does not clean the stove...you get the drift. This burned me up. I bet you could literally see smoke come out of my ears. I would give him an earful every time he washed the dishes. Afterward, he would continue to clean the kitchen "his way." One day I had an epiphany: the way he cleans the kitchen is not wrong; it is just different from mine. Therefore, if I don't like the way he does it, I can clean the kitchen myself from this day forward. That way of thinking changed our life. I stopped being his boss and proceeded to be his wife. This new method did wonders for my blood pressure and eliminated the animosity that had been building up between us for no reason. Instead of trying to make him the husband I wanted him to be, I began to work on being the wife that I needed to be. He didn't marry me to be his mother, but he married me to be his wife. Big difference. When I learned my role, I was able to play my part.

Step Three: Become a Cheerleader

Let's hear it for the boy
Let's give the boy a hand
Let's hear it for my baby
You know you got to understand

Deniece Williams, "Let's Hear It for the Boy" (1984)

As a former basketball player, there is nothing like hearing the roar of the crowd after you've made a killer move against your opponent. The crowd yelling your name after you've made the game-winning shot—the feeling is priceless. I brought that same attitude of gratitude over to my relationship. Whenever my partner does something good, I let him know that I appreciate it. For example, my husband tidied up the yard. I had to let him know how good of a job he did: "Look at this yard! It looks amazing. This looks like you hired a professional to do this. You have our home looking like a million bucks, baby." That statement was small but from the heart and highly effective. He couldn't wait to tidy up the yard again because he knew his wife was watching and appreciative.

Everyone loves to have their ego stroked. Your partner is no different. Dust off those pom poms and get that chant ready. If they committed a crime, we would be there with a bullhorn letting them know how much we disapprove of the behavior. The same goes for those that commit positive infractions. If they do something good, recognize them. If they said something witty, let them know how brilliant they are. All right, team, on three! One, Two, Three…

Step Four: Be Grateful

Thank you love
You made me happy in so many ways
Through all my sweet and tender yesterdays
You were the sunshine I needed love

Stevie Wonder, "Thank You Love," 1966

Have you ever held the door open for someone who was walking up right behind you, and they strolled on in as if you were not being courteous and you didn't exist. No "thank you," no "I appreciate it," or no "you don't have to," but they paraded in as if they were entitled to your door opening services. They acted as if you were obligated to be their personal bellhop. You wish you could reenact that moment and close the door directly in their face. Although the gesture was small, the individual fails to realize that no one is obligated to do anything for them. Everything done on their behalf is a courtesy. When my husband and I go to an event or out to dinner, I tell him "Thank you." Tradition demonstrates that it isn't uncommon for the spouse to foot the bill. It should be equally uncommon to relay an outward expression of thanks. With that being said, it is important to be thankful for everything. It literally starts at home.

According to Genesis 2:18, "It is not good that the man should be alone." Women are no different. Whether you realize it or not, no one is an island. Everybody needs somebody. With the utilization of these four steps, you are destined to keep a viable relationship together and respect the vows till death do them part. Everything that's worthwhile takes work—relationships included. If you are not ready to put in the work, you are not ready to be pronounced man and wife. Save your money and time. Moreover, save the time and the money of those whom wish you well. With some investigative dating, you will be in a better position to avoid the best thing you never had. And if you already took that leap, it may be time to date your spouse to determine how you can get a fresh start, either with or without them. But in all you do, remember the saying of the late poetess Maya Angelou, "If someone shows you who they are, believe them." It just may help you live your best life.

Lose to Win!

Melecia Scott

Laying side by side, reminiscing on the *mountaintop* moment that we both just experienced, we fully enjoyed this "winning moment."

"I love you," he whispers in my ear while his big strong arms stroke and caress me. "Babe, your skin is so soft, and you're just as beautiful as the first day when I met you. I love you so much, and I thank God for you being my *wife*!"

After 25 years of marriage and becoming wiser through our "losses," my husband and I are both ever so thankful to God the Father for re-igniting our physical appetites for one another and for climaxing our sexual intimacy to a new level. Understanding that in the bonds of marriage passionate lovemaking is truly beautiful, and only God and God alone has the ability and power to enhance it, elevate it, energize it, enrich it, and expand it into new depths.

Did you know that God is pro-sex? Yes, God is the one that created sex, and He created it to win as a beautiful expression of love between a man and a woman.

In the garden, when God told Adam and Eve to be fruitful and multiply, He also bestowed His divine approval and blessings upon it. Indeed, it was our omnipotent God that designed the body of a man and the body of a woman to fit jointly together. He made our bodies intrinsically unique and complementary one to the other, and His perspective on sex is no secret; all can be discovered in the Old Testament books, as well as the New Testament scriptures.

Today, my friend, it is our hopes to help you WIN again in your marriage by rekindling flames and igniting the fiery passion that you once had for each other. Yes, today, we want to help you "revive" and thrive in *every* area with your spouse! It is our prayer that YOU would begin to lay your marriage on the altar and believe for God to breathe life back into it. Do you that know God desires to be included in EVERY area of your marriage, even in the bedroom? King Solomon himself speak to couples through the Word of God, and he offers wisdom. Proverbs 5:19 says:

> Let her be as the loving hind and pleasant roe;
>   let her breasts satisfy thee at all time; and be
>   thou ravished always with her love.

Another scripture counsels us on how the husband is to love his wife:

> Husbands, love your wives, just as Christ
> loved the church and gave himself up for her.
>   (Ephesians 5:25)

First Solomon announces that the love of the wife is to refresh and fully satisfy her husband. And the second scripture emphasizes that the husband is to sacrifice for his wife, just as Christ made sacrifices for the church. In both scriptures' *sacrifices are made* because love requires sacrifice, and without sacrifices, the marriage will suffer. Ladies, for your marriage to "WIN," it's imperative for the wife to first **respect/honor** her husband, and secondly, she needs to understand that her body no longer belongs to her, but to her husband. And for the husband, he need to know, understand, and accept that he will be required to make daily sacrifices on behalf of his wife and his family!

To sacrifice means one must be willing to give of themselves in a variety of ways, and no marriage or relationship can succeed without it.

Many years ago, after my husband and I were married and the babies started coming, I thought to myself, "Dang! Is sex all he wants from me?" I was feeling like, "How many times a week do we have to do it?" Not understanding that through my **selfishness**, my marriage was slowly dying; I had a losing mindset.

As a newly married wife, this was all very "new" to me. Shoot, I was tired after taking care of my small kids; I didn't feel like having sex often. That was my mentality at that time. While we were dating, I didn't mind having sex with him all the time, even though sex before marriage is totally against the Word of God and His plan for sexual purity; however, I am just sharing my testimony and life experiences. So again, before Blake and I got married, we tested the waters many times. However, after marriage, we were not "WINNING" in the bedroom, in communication, or relationally, we were just feeling our way through miserably. Both of us had full-time jobs, and I was attending college at night, and all I wanted was sleep. Often, I was tired and just had no desire, but he did. Those first few years of marriage were very tough. We had to learn, grow, and get to know each other from a whole new perspective, embracing some habits and choices, and tolerating others. Nevertheless, through it all, God's grace was sufficient, and He began to shift our marriage, as we began learning from our many mistakes. Late in our marriage, God's power brought us to a place of surrender, and He empowered us to put selfishness and pride aside, teaching us how to serve one another humbly, and to daily trust Him to guide our footsteps on the path of victory. We understood that daily, every win, big or small, was a mark of victory. And always keep in mind that in the marriage game, what may look like a loss to others, just may be the greatest win for the marriage, so, appreciate the losses, learn from them, and empower others!

As we approach 27 years of matrimony, we are still striving to learn and grow, daily choosing to accept God's way of doing things because that path of unconditional love and sacrifice will always be better and beneficial for us in the end; we are abundantly grateful for each and every WIN, and we are as equally thankful for each and every loss. It was those losses that strengthened us and set us straight, ironically positioning our attitudes for the next WIN!

Here are some winning steps to help restore and rekindle your marriage:

1. Pray and fast earnestly for your marriage and for your spouse-keep both on the altar, even if he is not willing to pray with you.

2. Communicate with your spouse so that you both are in agreement to restore your marriage. Seek counseling if needed (through your spiritual leader or a professional).

3. Seek emotional healing/restoration from God for yourself. Speak the Word over yourself.

4. Refocus and shift your mindset through finding that spark that once attracted you to him in the beginning while yielding yourself to the Holy Spirit as He directs you toward change. Understand that while God is changing YOU, you need to wait patiently for God to make changes in your spouse. Try not to nag as you await the process. God can give you grace to do this.

5. Add spontaneity back to your marriage, take time out from the mundane of life to have fun, complement each other more, and begin appreciating the little things.

God is able to resurrect what was dead, or HE can re-birth something new! Just please know that He is ABLE! Ephesians 3:20

When "I do" Turns into "I don't"

Girl, Get Up and Win

Is It Worth the Ring?

Janice Freeman

Being married is supposed to be a beautiful union. I was married to a man I met in Long Beach, California. We had a great time together, and he was respectful, kind, and beautiful. He was in the military, born and raised in Texas, and we transferred to his hometown.

When we got to Texas, everything changed. He got together with some of his old buddies, and they were hanging out and drinking.

One night, he again wanted to go out, and I said, "OK, enjoy your night out with your friends."

The following day, he again went out to party with his friends, but he failed to leave me any money for groceries and other things we needed for the house. I had two young children at the time and was pregnant with my third, but I had to walk "miles" to the store. My husband and I had gone to the doctor together at one point, whereupon the doctor told both of us that mine was a high-risk pregnancy.

Two days later, he came home and said, "Go out there and clean the car." He knew I wasn't supposed to do that because of the pregnancy, but at that moment, I felt that I had to clean the car, or he would leave again, so I cleaned the car.

One night, he called me at two in the morning. He was in jail and asked me to bail him out. I said, "I don't have the money to get you out."

He got mad and said, "Call my grandfather for the money." I did so, and his grandfather posted bail. Then, he came home like nothing ever happened.

When he came home from jail, I noticed he didn't have his wedding ring on. I asked him about it, and he said the guard at the jail didn't give it back to him. That wasn't settled with my spirit. He lied to me about that. A week later, he wanted to go out again, and he asked me for his wallet. I told him I didn't know where it was, so he hit me, but I still couldn't tell him where it was because I had no idea.

After he left with his friends, I went to my neighbor's house next door and told her what had happened. She called the military police on base and reported the assault. When he arrived home, he was drunk and sleepy and passed out in bed. Then came the knock on the door. It was the military police. They took him to a certain location on base, and he made the choice to never come back to the house…or our marriage.

I was kicked out of base housing with two children while pregnant, and we slept in my car in the park and at different people's homes. My husband at the time didn't want me to work, so I had no money of my own.

I hired a divorce attorney who told me to stay in town until the divorce was final. So, I sent my children to my parents' house in California while I looked for work. It was very challenging. Thankfully, I found work as a CNA (Certified Nurse's Assistant) and cook at the county jail. Shortly thereafter, I ran into my ex-husband, whereupon he felt the need to tell me that he had slept with all of his female friends at work and at their place.

I was so incensed by this that I went out to the pier and thought about jumping. I felt ashamed and defeated because my marriage failed. I was bitter, angry, hurt, lost, and I didn't know how to face my family. Then, still on the pier, I heard a female's voice call out my name. "Janice! What are you doing?"

I didn't answer her, but she kept calling my name, and eventually, she caught up to me. No one knew I was there, but God! He sent her over to me so I wouldn't end my life. She was one of the military wives—a caring, good person.

I worked until I had enough money to pay for an attorney and a bus ticket back home. I prayed for God's protection through it all, as did my friend, the military wife. I left everything to him, got on that Greyhound bus, and never looked back.

She *Got Up!* to start over with her children.

In looking back at my experience, I realize I was in a place within myself saying, *Wow! Somebody wants to marry me.* He appeared to be a loving, kind, gentle, respectful man who cared about my family. But, as time went on, we moved out of state to Texas. That's when things started to change. It was his hometown friends and family. I experienced domestic violence, I was a *yes* wife to everything to hold my family together even though I was abused sexually, physically, mentally, emotionally, and verbally. I was caught up on the fact that a man wanted to marry me. When friends and family came around, I had to act like we were ok. He showed me the truth about himself during our marriage—eventually, I saw the truth and decided to follow *my own* truth.

Ladies, it is vital that you love yourself first! It's so important to know who you are and what you want. Set your standards! Just because a man smiles at you and says a few nice words in your ears doesn't mean he's the man. Take your time, pray, and wait on God. Follow the instructions of the Lord and trust Him! You are Blessed, Bold, and Beautiful! It's not ok to be abused in any way that is not love. I had to forgive myself, forgive him, and forgive my past so my healing could take place. It wasn't easy, but I had to go through my healing process to be a greater me. The Lord whispered and said to me on February 20, 2015, while I was on my healing bed, "GET UP AND WIN!" The whisper of the Lord saying "GET UP AND WIN" stayed in my heart and on my mind, and that helps me to continue to PUSH every day. I wrote a letter to myself to say I'm loving me. I'm not in a relationship right now because I want to experience the Hand of God in my relationship. I want God to introduce me to my husband to be. I went through the process of a cry to GET UP! I say this to myself every day: I LOVE ME! I'M LOVING LIFE! WIN!

#SHEGOTUP #YOUCAN2 #GETUPANDWIN
#GETUP! #STANDUP #WIN!

For the Love of Pete

Jules Cobb Edwards

As a little girl growing up in Lake City, South Carolina, in a house raised by my grandparents, I knew when I grew up, I wanted to be married to the man of my dreams, have a two-story house with a white picket fence, four girls (three of which were triplets), and a dog. I had it all planned out, well, at least I thought I did, then real life happened.

In December 1996, I made a decision that would change my life forever. I joined the United States Marine Corps. Prior to this decision, my life had no direction. I knew I wanted to be successful, but I had no idea how to do it. The Marine Corps not only gave me direction, it also gave me my husband…my Prince Charming, my Edward Lewis to Vivian Ward (characters from *Pretty Woman*). He was going to whisk me away, and we were supposed to live Happily Ever After.

Now, we are all old enough to know that life is hardly a well-written script for a hit movie. I met a man who was going to be my all and all, my right to my left, but we ended up being two left feet. Boy, was

I taken into a whirlwind! He was cute, sexy, and mine! Well, as you can see, I'm writing about surviving divorce, so that lets you know how this fairy tale ended.

When my ex and I divorced, I was broken. Probably the most broken I have ever been in my life. I honestly could not see why this had to happen to me and my family. Didn't God ordain marriage? Wasn't mine ordained? I couldn't figure it out. I must let you know that I cried, sobbed, mourned, and grew angrier for two years. Yes, twenty-four months of my life that I cannot get back I spent grieving the end of my three-year marriage.

One thing I will share is that in the aftermath of my divorce I realized that I was a horrible wife. While married, I would tell my husband that he was a want not a need, that I was going to file for divorce. For the love of Pete, I cannot tell you why I acted this way, but when the guacamole hit the fan, I wasn't prepared for the fallout. Now, by no means am I saying my ex was a Saint; I'm merely owning my part. Yeah, I was pretty rough at times. But I knew he wasn't going anywhere. Yeah, right! To pour salt in my bleeding wound, two weeks after the divorce was final, my father-in-law called to tell me that my ex had just married—to the woman he'd left me for. Talk about broken! I was broke, busted, disgusted, and depressed with three kids trying to figure out what to do with these millions of little pieces I had accumulated.

One of the hardest things that I had to come to terms with during this time was, why me? The most rhetorical answer I could give myself was "Why not you?" Funny thing is we ask God to send us the man that he has for us, and when the first one comes by and says he shares your dreams of family and life, we say thank you, Lord, I'll take him! Well, He didn't say *this* was the one. In fact, He showed me numerous times he was not in fact the man He had selected for me. I'll never forget walking down the aisle of the church I grew up in, knowing I was making one of the biggest mistakes of my life, but it was a little too late to turn back.

I remember hearing Bishop TD Jakes say, "When someone betrays your emotions, they become homeless. Sleeping under bridges with no place to go. It's not just when someone betrays you that relates to adultery, it's any time they prove they're not safe to love, and you have the unfinished business of loving them anyway. The torment you feel is the homelessness of love. While waiting for your heart to heal you have to allow the pain." That is just a deep quote to me.

Seventeen years later, the pain is gone; I no longer suffer the torment of the homelessness of love. The pain left an amazing scar. Every time I'm reminded of it, I thank God because I survived. That's right, I went from feeling tormented to being a survivor. While in the midst of being tormented by divorce, I didn't think I was going to make it. I didn't know *how* to make it to tell you the truth.

Here are a few things I learned throughout this process:

- God has a plan for your life.

Jeremiah 29:11, "For I know the plan I have for you," declares the Lord, "Plans to prosper you and not to harm you, plans to give you hope and a future" (NIV).

This verse alone tells me that though I got divorced, God still had a plan for my life. I would have a future full of hope and be successful.

- You need faith to live.

Hebrews 11:1, "Now faith is the substance of things hoped for, the evidence of things not seen" (KJV).

This is my favorite verse in the Bible. In my opinion, living without faith is not living. I had to believe and know that God would bring me out, that the pain would end, and I would love again. Every time I thought that I was a statistic, that no one would want me divorced with three children, I'd have to refer to this verse.

If you're going through a divorce or are divorced and having a hard time coping, I encourage you to pray and meditate on these verses. If God did it for me, He will surely do it for you.

Remember, For the Love of Pete, I made it through.

Knowing Your Worth in the Midst of Divorce

Monique Reynolds

Divorce is not what we think about when we think of marriage, and for some of us, we don't think about or consult God when we are getting married. For me, I married who I considered to be my friend, but I did not listen to the Holy Spirit when I felt in my spirit he was not the one. There were RED flags leading up to the wedding, and as some of us, we feel we can overcome these things if we press through. We become color blind, trying to see with blinders on. We become blind to the lies, excuses, cheating, and the list goes on. For me, he started out as a gentleman when he pursued me. During the engagement, there was talk of infidelity but no concrete evidence, but my gut said it was true, yet I ignored it. Trying to see the good in him. Some would say it's because there was no father in the home, and for some, that may be true. My father passed away when I was a little girl. Before he went home to be with the Lord, he instilled in me that I was beautiful, gifted, and talented. I was a princess, and I was strong. Even though my father was not there, I had brothers that continued to be that father figure for me.

Now, here I was, getting ready to walk down the aisle, my brother and I standing behind the doors, and he asked me if I had cold feet. I said to him, "I don't believe it is cold feet. I believe I may be making a mistake."

He told me I did not have to get married if I felt this way. I was thinking about the money that we spent and all the family and friends that were there. I was focused on the wrong things and not the things of God. The Bible says in Mark 10:9 (NASB) "What therefore God has joined together let no man separate." But God did not join us; this was not his perfect will for me. This was my permissive will, and God granted it. Again, my spirit was saying no, and I ignored it and married him in spite of. The wedding was beautiful, and my family and friends enjoyed themselves. The day after the wedding, ALL HELL broke loose. Family and friends were telling me of women he was with. I was devastated, hurt, and felt like a fool because I did not listen to what I've become to know as the Holy Spirit. As time went on, the marriage got worse. My body stated to tell the story of what was happening behind closed doors. I had doctors try to diagnose me with functional depression, but I refused to be depressed.

As time went along, I met a wonderful lady who befriended me and began to pray with and for me. She introduced me to a word teaching, Apostolic church that helped me through the process. During that time of being at the church, I began to cry out to

God for guidance and direction. I was lost and confused. At night, I would pray for hours, seeking the face of God concerning my marriage. I would have dreams of hitting a brick wall and did not understand the dreams at the time. I prayed that God would show me, tell me what I should do. You see you have to get people around you who will speak the word of God to you and pray with you, not speak on what they experienced. You see, he was not the man God had for me, so I didn't blame God. I took full responsibility for the storm that I was in. I must say I felt like Dorothy from the WIZ! Baby mama, infidelity, allegations of harassment, allegations of friends sleeping with my husband were tossed around and a whole other life across town.

Through prayer and seeking God's face, I was able to get through. I refused to have my kids see me unhappy, and I did not want my daughters to think it was ok to be in this type of situation. Speaking the word of God over my life, making declarations, and listening to Marvin Sapp's "Never Would Have Made It" helped me through that chapter in my life. I was healed until I moved to Texas and began going to my church Christ Purpose International Church. It was there that I found out I was not totally healed. That roots needed to be pulled up—that's when the transformation began. I forgave him fully, then I forgave myself. Healing and deliverance began to take place. Out of the storm, I rose. Out of the storm, I evolved. Out of the storm, I began to know who I am. Out of the storm, I was set free! My sisters, marriage is a wonderful thing when we allow God's will to supersede our will. When we become sensitive to God speaking to us. Allow God to mold you to the women he wants you to be. My sisters, rise and be the queens you are. God formed you from the rib of man; that means he took his time with you, molded you the way he saw fit, called you a Royal Diadem. Know your worth, know you are beautiful. My sisters, straighten your crowns, and if you see your sister's crown falling, help her. Here are a few declarations you can speak over yourself. Post on your mirror in the bathroom or on the refrigerator:

I AM courageous
I AM determined
I AM unstoppable
I AM victorious
I AM love
I AM gifted
I AM anointed
I AM blessed
I AM successful
I AM strengthened
I AM God's masterpiece
I AM whole
I AM confident
I AM forgiving
I AM well-able
I AM healed
I AM grateful

My sisters, allow God to minister to you and allow yourself to be healed. Sisters, come out of the storm and rise. Once I finish my declarations over myself, I say like Tiffany Haddish: "She Ready!"

The Payoff: Making Money Work for You

What Are Your Finances a Reflection Of?

Constance Craig-Mason

Have you ever felt like everything that you've ever wanted to be, do or have is so close? It's as if you're looking out of the window, and it's right there! But for some unknown reason(s), you cannot get the window open! Maybe you feel like there's an "invisible barrier" standing between you and your financial freedom? You just can't break the glass to walk into the fullness of all that is in store for you. So how do you get through that invisible barrier or open the window?

See, when you look at that window, you can see everything you want out there, right? The children playing outside of your beautiful, single-family home. You know the one with the huge yard, two car-garage, driveway, and the bay windows! Your spouse pulling into the driveway in a BMW 528i, next to your Infiniti Q50 that are both paid off. Amongst the mail that the mailman just left in the box is your quarterly retirement statement that shows over six figures invested, a bank statement of more than six months of expenses saved and a credit card statement from Discover with no payment due!

But you snap back to reality when someone cuts on a light from behind you. And now, instead of the imagery outside the window, you see something else in the glass. You see yourself, your reflection! That's not coincidental. That's the higher power shining the light on you, the things inside of you from your past and present that are holding you back. But what could it be? What do those things have to do with me getting my finances together and walking in financial independence?

Well, if you are anything like me, there was no inheritance that was passed down from generation to generation. No silver spoon to feed me with. From my great-grandmother, all the way down to me, there was no one in my immediate family who knew anything about financial concepts. I'm not talking about fancy terms like capitalism, return on investment, equity financing. I mean words like bank account, car insurance, budgeting, credit score! See, when you hear things like, "Make the ends meet," "Robbing Peter to pay Paul," "Broker than a joke," "Money doesn't grow on trees," and "I can't afford this," you think that struggle is normal. These statements are reflections of a poverty mentality, the mindset that there is never enough. And to be quite honest, self-damaging proclamations. Words have the ability to produce. For my spiritual queens, you may be familiar with the scripture that says, "Death and life are in the power of the tongue and those who love it will eat its fruit" (Proverbs 18:21).

Many of us who did not inherit a legacy of wealth and riches inherited the legacy of financial illiteracy. I am a firm believer that financial literacy is the key element in shifting the negative behaviors, habits, and emotions that impede our growth. The late author and motivational speaker Zig Ziglar said, "If you are not willing to learn no one can help you. If you are determined to learn no one can stop you." He also said, "Where you start is not as important as where you finish." And I'm sure that by now you have heard the quote, "Knowledge is power" by Sir Frances Bacon, right? I slightly disagree with him. I interpreted the quote to mean that knowledge is a key factor that "empowers" us to achieve great results. Instead of identifying what knowledge IS as a noun, I like to emphasize what it DOES as a verb. If I could change the quote, I would say, "Knowledge empowers." Empower means to enable, allow, authorize, equip, emancipate, unshackle, set free, liberate. According to the US Department of Education, 3.8 million American adult women have financial literacy skills below a basic (3rd grade) level. Wouldn't you agree that we need to prioritize financial liberation?

I remember being just 21 years old with three babies under the age of 4. The youngest of which was a premature baby boy, so I had to stay off from work for several months to nurse him to health. During that time, I had no income. The "Temporary Cash Assistance" that I had applied for through my local Department of Social Services took about three months to finalize. Once those funds arrived, I had to pay it all out in an effort to "catch up" on my rent and other monthly expenses. Once my son was stable enough to go to daycare, I scurried to find employment. I found a job but resigned after two months due to sexual harassment from my immediate supervisor. I sought out many other job opportunities. I was super excited about a new job that I was hired for. It paid just $9.00 per hour (back in 2000).

Because I had Googled instructions on how to get out of debt, I learned that communicating with creditors and making payment arrangements would help. I wrote a letter to a creditor explaining my situation and stated that I could afford $38.75 monthly for 24 months. I did that with all the creditors I had at the time. My total debt was only $7,000, but to me, it was so debilitating. I still have that letter to this day! It reminds me of how far I have come, and that no matter what happens, I must have financial integrity. I read everything that I could about money to improve my financial situation. What I learned, I shared with my family, friends, coworkers, practically everyone who would listen! I had no idea that nine years later, I would start a journey toward becoming a passionate, financial professional fueled with the purpose of helping to break the chains of financial illiteracy in communities. And now 19 years later, I can share my story with queens like you of how I went from an unemployed, single mom living in poverty to a happily married, international, financial expert speaker! Hardship was a catalyst for a life shift toward a positive, financial well-being.

Financial well-being is a state of being where a person can fully meet current and ongoing obligations, feel secure in their financial future, and is able to make choices that allow them to enjoy life. In short, it's a reflection of how financially confident you are now and for the future. Do not be ashamed if you aren't feeling that confident. According to the Federal Reserve, 40% of Americans do not have enough cash to pay an unexpected bill of just $400. And nearly half of Americans couldn't come up with $2,000 in 30 days to handle an unexpected expense per the National Bureau of Economic Research. The steps that it takes to go from financially frustrated to financially liberated are not very complicated. However, it will require that you do the work! For my spiritual queens, "Faith without work is dead!" (James 2:18)

Firstly, you need to get clear. Make a conscious choice to improve your financial status. Believe that you are worthy of so much more. Life is full of possibilities, and you were created to win! Remember when I asked you about looking through the window and seeing the possibilities, but feeling stuck once you saw yourself in the reflection? Believe it or not, reflecting is a very beautiful, vulnerable, critical next step. Think about the ways you may have self-sabotaged your funds or savings. If you have had some retail therapy or emotional spending days, you are not alone! To help narrow down your true financial status, pull out your bank and credit card statements. Don't judge, just review, making note of income, expenses, and areas where you may need to make adjustments.

The next step that I recommend is getting an accountability partner such as an experienced financial coach. This professional will teach you how money works, help you identify and break negative emotions, behaviors and habits that have held you back. The coach will also help you plan and strategize your short-term and long-term financial goals such as emergency funding, projects, buying a home, etc. He or she may also be able to refer you to other financial professionals, as needed, such as certified financial planners (CFPs), certified public accountants (CPAs), personal bankers, insurance agents, mortgage loan officers, and the like. If you are unable to obtain a financial coach, the Consumer Finance Protection Bureau (CFPB) and the Federal Trade Commission (FTC) offer a vast array of free online resources to help you educate yourself.

And lastly, but certainly not the least step, garner an unwavering level of determination and persistence. Dig deep, and no matter what comes your way, you will endeavor to stay the course. Consistency is king or, in this case, queen!

Broke But Not Busted: Changing Lanes and Moving Forward from the Pit of Debt

Tywauna Wilson

*There are no shortcuts when it comes to getting out of debt. -
Dave Ramsey*

I remember it like it was yesterday. I went from having decent credit with the ability to get whatever I wanted to poor credit and needing a co-signer…just like that. I had graduated from college and moved back home with my mom to get on my feet and start working my new job as a medical laboratory scientist. I wanted to stack some money before getting a place of my own and starting true independence of life after college. I wasn't make making a lot of money, but it was sufficient for me to get started on considering I had no experience in my field. My income covered my student loans, car note, and cell phone bill, and I was able to save a little to move into my own place. Life was good or so I thought until I received a small pink card from the post office requiring my signature.

The post office had already closed for the evening, so I had to wait until the next business day to go and sign for this certified mailing. I really didn't know what it was, so I had a little angst because someone I didn't know was sending me a certified package. The next day, I went to the post office and received the letter. I opened it up, only to find out a creditor was suing me for over $4,000, and there was a date for me to appear in court! I thought, there has got to be some mistake. I read further down, and it was from one of the two credit cards I got while I was in college. I had blocked it out of my mind that I didn't pay them, but clearly they remembered. I needed those cards...I had good intentions. Coming from a low-income household, even with the grants, scholarships, student loans, and my working part-time, it was still not enough to cover the expenses. Those credit cards helped me get through to pay for tuition and books. Why didn't they understand that? Now outside of school expenses, I must admit, I did buy some new clothes and took a spring break trip, but that was part of the college experience, right? My intentions were good, and I started out strong; however, the ability to pay the monthly statement was becoming a burden, so I stopped paying. After I graduated from college, I didn't hear from them, so I quickly forgot. It seemed like we were all good because for years I never heard anything about the debt, so naïve me figured that I no longer owed it. Boy was I wrong. I quickly learned that out of sight does not mean out of mind.

Finally, it was court day, and I was nervous. I didn't know how the system worked. Before I was to appear before the judge, I went into preconference to see if I and the other party could work out a deal. We did, and the outcome was a payment plan option. No reduction in the debt but an agreed upon monthly plan. We settled, and I was relieved, thinking it was all over. Well that part was over, but my credit score took a nose dive once the judgment hit my credit report. Several months went by, and I was getting settled into my new role, paying my monthly expenses, and I received another pink card in the mail. You have got to be kidding me, I thought. As you may have guessed, the other creditor from college had followed suit with another $3,000 debt with another monthly commitment. I was now at credit score of poor. The shame and the rejection you feel when you can't get the apartment you want, new job opportunities, or other essentials because you don't meet the "standard" can mentally destroy you. My degree couldn't save me. In this case, I felt like it put me in this situation. I didn't know anyone with access to that kind of money to do me a favor, so I had to figure something out. I had to hit the lottery! Well that's easier said than done and considering the odds, that option was a no go. I thought about working with a company that would consolidate all of my debt, and I'd pay them monthly. I was advised this would hurt more than it would help. The options were few, and there was no running away and avoiding this. I had to put on my big girl panties and work off my debt or the long term outcome would have detrimental consequences and wage garnishment impact.

The sacrifice to climb out of this hole was serious. I came up with a monthly budget to pay all of these bills and a three-year plan to have at least the creditors paid off. I had very little left over for entertainment or shopping but to escape the feeling of disgust and limited access, I was willing to do whatever it took to turn this around. I picked up extra shifts to help pay down the debt faster. There were a few times where the funds didn't add up, and I had to go to the check exchange. Avoid those kind of places at all cost if possible! It is hard as heck to get out of that vicious cycle. I kept at it though as I was determined not to let this break me. I wanted access, I wanted options, I wanted nice things, I wanted opportunities and all the other possibilities that come along with having good credit.

Over the next few years, all I did was work, sleep, eat, and pay my bills on time. Not a fun or luxurious time at all. I was committed to doing the work. It was my own actions that got me there in the first place. I would pray, Lord, please get me through this. Help me! Within two and a half years, I was able to pay off those debts and began to slowly rebuild my credit. After that, I began to save as I didn't want to be caught in that kind of situation again. In seven years, I went from poor credit to an over 800 credit score. It was a blessing! I learned that there are no short cuts or easy fixes in life. Hard work and sacrifices will have to be made in order to achieve those things that are important to you. When you know better, you do better. So, girl, you may be feeling broke, busted, and thinking there is no way you can keep the walls from caving in. We all make decisions that we feel are in our best interest at the time, only to find out later it would come at a cost. From one winner to the next, it's never too late to change the narrative. So go ahead, girl, and get up and win!!

Breaking the Darkness of Depression

The Importance of Getting Up and Doing Something

Cassie Catlett

As I stood there naked staring at my body, I thought, what now? I was disgusted. I didn't see strength. I didn't see faith. I didn't see hope. I didn't see resiliency. I saw scars, lots and lots of scars. I saw no children, no breast, no future, no love, and no desire. I saw all the photos and movie scenes with sexy desirable women flash before me, and I knew it would never be me again. I would not be the picture any man imagined in his mind ever again... How did I get here? Did I do this? Was this my fault? Everything I had been taught from birth about being a woman, and a desirable one at that, since that's what seemed to matter most to those around me, was now gone! As I looked at myself in the mirror, all I saw was fear, insecurity, hatred, disgust, and weakness.

I need you to understand this isn't just about cancer. Sure, most of the physical scars were from cancer. The scariest part was that I had somehow survived everything to be standing there thinking my worth to the world was physical and sexual and somehow defined mostly by men and not at all by me. After so many years of therapy, I was still allowing everything I had been through to define me, to weaken me, to stop me… GET UP, GIRL!

You see, I knew how to have an orgasm before I ever kissed a boy. I grew up being molested by my grandfather. I don't remember a time in my childhood when he wasn't touching me. I don't remember thinking it was weird, I really don't remember thinking anything of it, until I was gang raped by some cousins. Yes, all this by the age of 10. WTF? That's exactly what I thought later in life when I realized what I had actually lived through. The truth is though, when you grow up around all this and it's happening to you, you don't really think much about it. I must have known somewhere deep within me that something was wrong, but survival instincts are astonishing; they truly work. Many times I have thought, how fortunate I was that I didn't know anything was wrong. You see I was a happy child, shy and timid, but happy. Of course, now I understand that my shy, timid, sensitive nature was pure FEAR and a truly understandable fear.

Please understand I love my family; they did the best they could. Of course, hindsight is 20/20, and I now understand my mom and dad had their own set of problems and demons they were constantly fighting. The minute they found out about my grandfather, not by me of course, they stepped in and never had me be around him again unless I wanted it. I did though—go around him again as I became a master people pleaser, the loyal one, and the pretty one. The later would become the theme of my life.

I have been fortunate and brave enough to stand face to face with each one of my abusers. I have forgiven them. I know they were sick. It was never about me. I did nothing to deserve it or bring it on. Mental illness is real, and I've seen it up close and personal. The beginning of the end started when I saw one of my younger cousins doing something that set off a gut reaction I'll never be able to fully explain. I knew, within seconds, that my grandfather was touching her. I told. When I say I told, I mean I went to the police station and filed actual allegations against my grandfather. Yes, it was a big deal. I was 14. I have no idea how I ever got the courage to do that. I barely remember it to this day. All I knew was that if he ever touched my baby sister, I'd probably kill him and go to jail, ok probably not. I did know that I would feel like an accomplice if it ever happened to her. I learned later that he had abused other people, but no one ever told, so he kept doing it. If they had told, maybe it wouldn't have happened to me, but it was too late for me. It was not too late for my sister though, so he had to be stopped. He was. No, he didn't go to jail; after so many years, no one cares about molestation, which is crazy to me because it affects the survivor for the rest of their lives! There were consequences though; he went to counseling, and I was not allowed near that side of my family anymore.

Me? I was the ostracized one. My Christmas presents were left at the back door. I was the jerk that told the family secret. When my grandmother died, I tried to make peace with the family. I loved her. I missed her. She was my idol. I looked like her. I never blamed her. As the loyal good girl, I tried to keep the peace, bring us all together, show everyone that everything was just fine now. Then the dreaded day happened…my grandfather attempted to make things right with me. He apologized for all he did, then he said the thing I will never ever forget and oddly the thing that helped me forgive him the most, "But you didn't wear panties. What was I supposed to think?"

HOLY SHIT. He tried to kiss me again after that, and I walked away and never saw him again. I didn't hate him anymore though; I felt sorry for him. He was sick! He thought a 4-year-old was seducing him. That's an illness, end of story. I don't regret any of it; my cousin got help right away. He never touched my sister. It was worth it all. Most importantly, I finally knew it wasn't me. I was FREE. Forgiveness gave me a kind of freedom that nothing else ever has.

So how, after all that, was I standing in front of a mirror still somehow allowing the world to define me? How did I still see my worth as a woman and a person, as only being physical and sexual? There I was on my 33rd birthday, taking my mastectomy bandages off, surrounded by people who loved me, yet feeling alone and afraid and completely unaware of my worth. How the hell did this end up here? GET UP, GRIL!

I didn't have some grand spiritual awakening. I know many who have, but it wasn't me. I had a series of events that piece by piece broke me far enough down to finally decide I had to make a change. My dad had been diagnosed with cancer a year before my breast cancer diagnosis and was losing his battle. Fifteen days after he passed, one of my best friends of

20 plus years took her own life. This was the final straw for me. I knew that a huge part of why she did this was because her relationship had ended, and her self-esteem and dependence were so deeply rooted in that relationship that she felt she had nothing else when it was over. That triggered something in me that had been brewing for quite some time. I had been working on me and getting my life back, my sexy back, but what I now knew with every core of my being was I had to help other women do the same. I needed to Re-Define Womanhood! I needed to Re-Define Sexy! I would be the one! Instead of waiting for someone to come rescue me from the life I felt trapped in, I decided I would rescue me, and I would show other women how to do the same. I will be the HERO of my story, and I will teach you how to be your Hero. GIRL, STOP JUST GETTING BACK UP. NOW GET UP AND DO SOMETHING!

Recently, I posted a picture of my breast with my new dragonfly tattoo covering my mastectomy scars. In almost every part of the world, the dragonfly symbolizes change, self-realization, a mental and emotional maturing and an understanding of the deeper meaning in life. I did it for a number of reasons, some of which seem obvious. Scars are beautiful, and I haven't covered up all of mine, but I was sick of looking at sickness because that's what we see when we, and I mean cancer survivors, look at our scars. We see CANCER. We know most of you don't. We hear you when you say how strong and courageous we are, but what I have learned is that what you think of me and how you feel about me is not my business, nor can I afford to allow it to affect me anymore, good or bad. Beauty is on the inside.

We've heard this so many times it appears to have lost its impact. It may be the most important thing you learn to embed into your innermost soul though.

A few years ago, I had a great discussion with my ex-husband, the one who left me for my best friend while I was going through breast cancer—oh, I may not have mentioned that. lol Why? Because the truth is, it is not significant anymore. What he did was a reflection of him, not me. I learned that. I was able to tell him that I forgave him many years before he asked for forgiveness. I've learned that if I have not been in your shoes, I have no business judging you, and frankly it only kills my soul when I can't forgive someone. I said earlier that forgiveness gave me a sort of freedom that nothing else has. The only thing that has impacted my life as much if not more than forgiveness is LOVE. Loving you as you are and loving me where I am. Loving my past mistakes. Loving my past hurts. Loving all the ugly truths about me and loving all your ugly truths. For it is through love and forgiveness that one is truly awakened to the eternal sunlight of the spirit. Happiness is a choice and one that I choose to make every day. Today, I stand tall, proud, happy, and sexy as hell, for I have not just survived the darkness, I have shone a light on it that cannot and will not ever be dimmed again. May you find that light that is buried deep within you begging to shine. GET UP, GIRL, AND WIN!

Girl, BREATHE: How I Handled Depression!

Sandra Mizell Chaney

Ms. Mizell, do you know where you are? Do you know why you are here?

These are the questions that greeted me as I woke up in the hospital. Depression is very REAL, yawl! How about I did not really realize I was depressed? I would walk around saying I'm sad, I'm tired, I'm mentally drained, and so forth and so forth. ANYHOO, my depression led me to attempt suicide. During that season of my life, I was divorced, a single parent, a survivor of several abusive relationships, in a relationship that was not good for my soul and working in corporate America. Everyone who knew me during that season, including colleagues, always complimented me on how strong and put together I looked. Yet I on the inside, I was so sad and crying. Can anyone relate?

Being a survivor of domestic violence and sexual assault gave a place to hide from my depression. Of course I did not see that at the time. I mean who wouldn't be depressed after dealing with that? Besides, I never heard of anyone saying I'm a survivor

99

or conqueror of depression. You do hear I am a survivor or conqueror of domestic violence. Mental health issues are considered taboo. No one wants to have authentic conversations about it. I often wondered why that was so. Then I realized it has to start with self. I am very grateful for my counselor who initiated that conversation. This was my first lesson in breathing. Let me become vulnerable enough to open my heart and share. It at least will start a conversation and help me to peel back another layer of my onion. Girl, BREATHE! WHEW!

Growing up, there was always that kid that everybody talked about and labeled crazy because it appeared he or she had some mental health issues. Nobody wanted to be associated with that, right? Well, I could relate to that kid. I remembered being sad a lot, but not showing it or wanting to cry, but would hear "Stop that crying before I give you something to cry about." I learned how to keep things in and pretend all was well while growing up. There was so much chaos going on in my life, even as a kid. So I learned how to be the peacemaker or at least in my mind that's what it looked like. I would pretend that my life was okay. I never spoke of things that were going on in the negative. I carried all of that into adult hood. I became the strong and responsible one. I wore that badge with honor. As a black women working in corporate America, I needed to be strong, I could not show any vulnerability or signs of weakness. What's funny to me about this is when REALLY angry tears started to flow. When that happened, World War 3 was about to start. I managed to only do this in my personal life. In my business life, I was the peacemaker and pretended all was well.

So what does all of this have to do with depression? A lot! Let's not forget the week before the menstrual cycles – WHEW! Girl, I am PMSing all over the place. Depression is hot and heavy then. Did you know that hormonal imbalances like issues with pregnancy, menopause, and perimenopause can send you into depression? I did not know that. Again, I would always use the word sad to describe what I was going through. Sadness did not necessarily mean I was depressed. It just meant I was sad. So, when I had my hysterectomy in my late twenties, early thirties (don't know the exact age), I went through a deep depression. I did not know it at the time. I started thinking about everything: being divorced, a single parent, being in a relationship not good for me, I can't have kids, my womanhood is now gone, etc. Yes, that last one was major for me. It sent me into this tailspin of a deep hole that I did not how to get out of. So attempting suicide was my only answer. I did not have anyone to talk to about what was happening. Remember, mental health issues are not talked about. To add to this, I was dealing with everyday stress issues, so that to me was my only relief.

Well, THANK GOD for miracles. They very relationship that was not good for me saved me. I ended up in the hospital, waking up to questions such as "Ms. Mizell, do you know where you are?" I stayed in the hospital for a few days. I then ended up in a residential treatment facility for 30 days and on anti-depressants for a while.

Being in this facility taught me how to breathe again and be vulnerable. I had stopped breathing. I was the energizer bunny. I just kept going and stuffing things down, and one day I just had enough. During that stay, I learned so much about me like I was depressed, apparently for a long time.

Here are some symptoms I had. Maybe you can relate to a few, especially if you have had them consistently.

- Feelings of emptiness, hopelessness, despair, and sadness
- Irritability, anxiousness, and guilt
- Feelings of exhaustion, severe tiredness
- Loss of interest in previously pleasurable activities
- Inability to concentrate or remember details
- Suicidal thoughts or attempts of suicide
- Sleep disturbances –sleeping too much or too little
- Changes in appetite – eating too much or too little
- Physical symptoms – aches and pains, cramps, headaches, digestive issues, breast tenderness, bloating
- Lack of energy

Depression is not a sign of weakness. It really is a sign that something is wrong, and it is okay to acknowledge it and seek help. These symptoms did not just pop up one day and say, "Hello, here I am." They happened gradually. Remember, this started when I was young. This may not be your story. Maybe it started for you when you were in adulthood. Maybe it's just a hormonal imbalance. The body speaks. Listen to it.

ANYHOO, what I know now is I was depressed and unaware. I don't want my sisters to be unaware or suffer in silence anymore. Girl, it's time to truly BREATHE! So that is what I did!

So let me tell you how I handled my depression. After the suicide attempt and while in the residential facility, which, by the way, was in a beautiful six-bedroom house in nature (but God), I started on the road to healing my mind and soul. Here is what I did:

1. I entered into therapy. Of course, it was a part of my treatment plan, but I knew this was what I needed. I participated fully in the process. Please go to therapy, if necessary. It really is a good thing. I will say this, having the RIGHT therapist is important. Having someone to help you navigate your thoughts and feelings is vital to your mind, body, and spirit.

2. I acknowledged that I really was depressed. That meant I needed to be vulnerable, I needed to open my heart, I needed to be honest with myself, and I needed to put voice to it and not hide from it. You cannot heal what you won't acknowledge. If you are unaware or unsure, check in with a professional to see where you are.

3. I get at least seven hours a sleep a night, and I take naps when I can. I found when I did not get enough sleep through the week it affected my emotional state and how I handled things. Overtime, the effects of team no sleep become magnified with everything else going

on. I am important! You are important. Get some good sleep. It works wonders!

4. I LOVE the beach or just being near water. I am able to exhale and just be. I can just let go and release.

5. Just getting outside in the sun. Them vitamin Ds are the bomb.com. Get out in the sun. Just get out of the house. Do something for you.

6. I exercise, I do yoga, regularly; I move my body. I love to dance, too. I take dance breaks in the middle of the day because I love music. When you move your body, it clears stagnant energy.

7. Remember to BREATHE! Your breath will save you! I make a conscious effort to feel my breath. That means I must stop what I'm doing to check in with me, and my breath helps me with that.

I think you get the point. Don't ignore what you are feeling. Do not allow the stigma that society has placed on mental health keep you in a state of pretending everything is okay. Your strength lies in your vulnerability. That is where the true healing can begin. Girl, BREATHE!

Let Your Trials Make You BETTER Not Bitter

Dianna Forsberg

In December of 2016, I came to the realization that my marriage of six and a half years was coming to an end. I wholeheartedly wanted the kind of marriage that would stand the test of time and the loving family my son deserved. However, his dad and I had reached the point of no return. I filed for divorce right before the new year. We fought over property, cars, money, and custody of Dillon. This was a tumultuous one and half years to say the least, until the divorce was finalized. In the process of waiting for the divorce to be finalized, I moved into my own apartment. I found myself coming short on cash due to the high-cost attorney bills and money being tied up in the divorce.

But, September of 2017, I found an additional stream of income that saved my life. I said to myself, "WOW, finally a relief and a cushion."

Fast forward to January of 2018 when after 15 years in corporate America as an engineer for Nokia, I was laid off. Here I was a single mother going through a messy divorce, fighting for custody of my two-year-old son, and now laid off from work. My days and nights were mentally tough. I wasn't receiving child support, and I knew that everything would rest on my shoulders. It was tough for many days, but I quickly learned that the fight wasn't with anyone else. The fight was within. I had restless nights, but I used that time to build my team, build my business, and grow my own personal health and wellness brand. While being an engineer, I served in the health and wellness industry for eight years. Now, it was time to build it full-time. The more I would immerse myself into personal development and surround myself with people who were more successful than I, the stronger I would become.

My mindset was *I am going to WIN despite what I am going through. I don't care what my situation looks like, I am going to walk in faith and operate with a winning spirit. This is how I will survive this.* Very quickly, I was growing as an individual, a mother, and a business owner. In 2018, I made media appearances on two major television networks, a radio interview, three magazine features and was chosen as a health and wellness coach for a large women's conference. I also had a few more projects in the works.

I was happy and excited, but there was a dark cloud over my head. The divorce was still lingering. One night as I was lying in bed, I had an epiphany. I began to ask myself if the fight in the divorce was a real fight or if it was my ego? In my mind, I did everything I could to save my marriage. I wasn't at fault. Why should I give up money and possessions that were rightfully mine? That night, God spoke to me. I knew that everything I thought I was losing in the marriage could be and would be replaced. So, what was I fighting for? I had to check myself. That night, I realized I had wasted one and half years fighting because of my ego. That was the night I decided the fight was over. The next morning, I got on my attorney's calendar to inform her that I no longer wanted to fight. My precise words to her were, "Give him everything he wants." She looked at me and responded, "Dianna, he wants $20,000. I don't think you should give in." I said, "I'm sure about this. God told me it's over and to let it go." She submitted a new divorce decree that put everything in his favor. After receiving the new decree, he called me and said, "Dianna, it's okay. I don't want anything anymore. Let's just be reasonable splitting everything. I'm tired of fighting, too." It was another defining moment that year where I realized sometimes we are fighting with egos, and egos are causing us more pain through our situations. I was grateful for prayer, my personal development time, and my obedience to God to just trust him.

In October of 2018, my son's nanny who had been with us for two years of his life had a contract that ended and was returning to the Philippines. This woman was a huge part of the family who loved and treated my son like her own and was essentially a second mother to him. I knew this transition would not be easy, and I was heartbroken. The days leading up to her last day of departure had me in tears. Two weeks prior to her departure, her replacement arrived, and all seemed well. The interviews with her over Skype were great. She seemed happy, knowledgeable, and excited. After three weeks of her arrival, I noticed a difference in her attitude toward my son. I wasn't immediately concerned, but both I and Dillon's dad observed the same behaviors.

In early November, while driving home from the grocery store with Dillon and the new nanny, I was going through a green light, looked up, and a car was trying to make a U-turn and was directly in front of my car, causing a head-on collision. It happened so quickly I had no time to avoid it. I was in shock, Dillon was screaming, and the nanny was frantic. I was taken by ambulance while I listened to my baby screaming for his mama, and there was nothing I could do but lay still and cry. My car was totaled. I suffered a severe concussion and major back and neck spasms. I was again reminded of the mental strength that was needed to be an entrepreneur and a single mom with no child support. How was I going to get through this period? How long am I going to be down on my back like this? How am I going to run my businesses? How am I going to ensure my bills are paid AND keep investing toward expenses to build my brand through this rough patch? I was stressed to the max once again. A few weeks past and over the course of three days, I watched and listened to my son's new nanny verbally, mentally, and physically abuse my son. I confronted her and called the agency immediately. I was going through every emotion imaginable. Here I am sick with a concussion that has me sleeping constantly, can barely hold my son due to muscle spasms, stressed about my livelihood, and now stressed about my son's caregiver.

I can recall one morning—I called my best friend crying so hard. I said, "Something isn't right with me. I feel like I am losing my mind. I feel lower than the ground." She listened to me, and she responded, "I know you. You are stronger than anyone I know. You just need to get this cry out, and you will be fine. You bounce back from everything." Shortly after we hung up, mentally, I did feel better. That warrior spirit came over me once again. I said to myself, "I have no idea how all of these things are going to work out, but you know you don't have the luxury to fall apart. Get it together." Day by day, step by step, decision after decision, prayer after prayer, things started to come together. Daily personal development and prayer reshaping my mind from negative thoughts to positive thoughts. The more time I spent reflecting and asking God for guidance, the more he began to show me this pause in my life was necessary. There were some things and people I was holding on to that couldn't go into the new year if I was ready to move to the next level. God revealed them as clear as day. I obeyed and I released them.

Within weeks, my therapy was getting so much better that I could lift weights and most days without pain. I received a call regarding a project that had been put on hold due to my accident. The project was put back on the calendar for the coming year, and I received an email that I would be honored in a ceremony for "Who's Who of Black Dallas." I received peace in my heart and mind; God gave me a new vision for a project, and my businesses started booming again. This year, I will finally launch my fitness apparel line, I will release my first book this summer, and I have started an initiative called Project 1000 of my 30-day water challenge. I will help 1,000 people lose 10 lbs. in 30 days on my water challenge in 2019. It has been an incredible challenge where clients are dropping between 10-18 lbs. within 30 days naturally. This movement will change so many lives.

I have relied more on hope, faith, prayer, and personal development in the past few years than I have in my entire life. The combination has been the key to growing, accepting responsibility, recognizing areas of weakness, and being eager to improve. We cannot get to our next level in life if we cannot accept our current level of faults and be ready to make corrections. Sometimes, life can have you so busy that you aren't recognizing or even wanting to accept when you need to change. It takes hardship, heartache, and tough times to reshape and sharpen us into better people. Upon waking up, I pray and then spend a minimum of 30 minutes reading or listening to personal development. When I have a challenging day, I might dig into personal development 2-3 times within the day.

I would like to encourage you to first identify where and what you lack. Write it out on paper. Be honest with yourself. You can't improve if you can't accept your reality. Your next move MUST be your BEST move. It starts with self-reflection. What are your 30-60-90 day goals? What do you want out of this game called life? What are you willing to sacrifice to get it? Your greatest asset and power are your DISCIPLINE and SACRIFICE. Every time I won a battle, it was because I made the decision to sacrifice and apply discipline to my life. You might sacrifice your "free time," watching TV, hanging out with friends, that extra 1-2 hours of sleep, that healthy meal over an unhealthy meal, that workout session even when you don't feel like it. Just know that victory is on the other side of what "feels hard" now. Start your day with prayer/meditation, reviewing your goals, and putting in the work daily to accomplish them. It will take extreme focus. Anything that doesn't put you closer to your goal or isn't a part of your future must be eliminated. That includes things, activities, and people. No exceptions. If it doesn't put you closer to your goal, you must omit it. Apply these practices daily and be prepared to absolutely crush every goal imaginable.

Short term sacrifice to be a champion for the long term.

Girl, Take Your Medication

DaMesha M. Jackson

Really quickly, I want to explain something to the women, especially black women because in our culture, it has become taboo to discuss mental health, and even more so when you belong to the Christian faith. This has become problematic because while we sit silently on the sidelines, black women suffer, and some have even lost their lives. People tell you, you have to be a strong black woman, or that's life, or even suck it up. It happens in the church, too: you're not depressed, it's the devil, it's a spirit, you don't need a counselor, you need Jesus. I am here to tell you, whether you believe those things or not, you may need a counselor, and if you have been given medication, take your medication!

Nothing is worse than having to walk around like a shell while trying to figure out how other people's thoughts, feelings, emotions, and advice play into your life. You only have one life to live to your best advantage, so until you figure out if it's just demons, or even while trying to get closer to God, take your medication. Your mind, body, and your family will thank you! Because while people form opinions of your situations and solutions for your problems that they may not have never encountered, you are suffering in silence instead of silencing the voices and opinions of others.

You could be like me; you know all the right things to do to enhance your life, you can know that you want to live better and free and smile and laugh but still not have the mental capacity to do any of those things. See, I know what that's like. I know what it's like to be stuck between my religion and my mental health, to be stuck between society and my mental health, to be stuck between stereotypes and my mental health; I know how it is to just be stuck. But, what we as women have to realize is that just as much as we value others' opinions, at the end of the day, we have to do what is best for us, whatever that is—even if that means seeing a therapist, taking medication, and even cutting off toxic people in our life, which may include family and friends.

Since dealing with depression, I have made an awesome discovery. I've received great advice from my family and friends, but I'm the one who has to sleep with myself at night. I have to sleep with my thoughts, my emotions, and my decisions every night. I have to be content and happy with everything I do, knowing it was the best decision I could make at the given time. So we need to start putting ourselves first, and that may mean taking medication. Even if you are strong in the faith, and yes, I have been that person.

You will have moments. Moments where it doesn't look good right now, I don't see it looking good, I know the word, but for some reason, my mind can't grasp what the other side looks like right now. And you know, that's ok. Before those thoughts become too bad to bear and you feel completely hopeless, I encourage you to take your medication. At least until your faith becomes stronger and full circle because it will give you just enough to make it through the day, or the night. For me, it was enough to make sure that I would be here for my children; I took my medication for them. Yes, I was scared, unsure, felt like I was giving up on my faith, felt like I was not a real Christian, but none of that mattered. What mattered at the moment I decided to take my medication was realizing that I had two little people waking up expecting to see me the next morning. I couldn't go out like that. I had to defy the odds and go against basically everything I knew to overcome depression. A strong support system is great and beautiful, but I needed to make that decision for myself. I knew how bad my mental state was, I knew how hard it was to cook, be social, and be there for my children while not taking my medication. Don't let anyone tell you that the actions you plan take will not work for you. Just like women's intuition tells you when something is up with your man, it also tells us when something is not right within ourselves. Listen to that small inner voice. She knows what's best. Regardless of what your friends and family say, you have to do what's best for you. Even if it seems like the road less traveled, do it anyway. It just may be the best road for you. Take it from a person who fought her way through. From a person who has been to the bottom of the barrel, who has seen the dark side. Make the right choice before it's too late. You don't need everyone's support; you just need to take that one step in the right direction.

Girl, take your medication. Worry about what people may say later, or better yet not at all. Those who don't support any and every decision you make to better yourself, cut them off. Only you truly know what's best for you deep down inside. You may already be in the place you are at because of how others have made you feel and what they have said, so don't include them in your healing. Let them wonder, and when they see you, they will know that they are inferior to your power to work things out for yourself. They may even be amazed at your resiliency to comeback after almost losing your life. There is no way I would have been able to say this to anyone in May of 2018. I was that girl in the beginning of the story who listened and watched others. I loved living my life through other people's lens and basing my desires on what others had because it worked best for them, not thinking that maybe God had something different and greater for me. I was just thinking that he had forgot. I rationalized my reality with someone else's and traded the genuine inner voice of my strength for voices of others' opinions and advice that worked for them but not for Mesha.

See, when people asked me what I wanted, my response was, "Well, my friend got this, and they did that. I can try to do this or that like them, and why is it not coming to me like it came to them?" I didn't realize that I dug my own grave, and in May of last year, those same voices and thoughts of others were going to take me out of here. Never in a million years did I want to end up at the bottom of the barrel, really up under the barrel, but there I was, suicidal, depressed, lonely, and confused. I wasn't sure about…anything at that time. But what I did do for myself is I sought treatment. I started to consistently see a therapist, and you know what? I began to take medication. My goal was not to be on it long, but just long enough to get myself stable again, to go out and laugh again, and to enjoy my life to the fullest!

Taking medication didn't make me feel like a "sellout" or make me feel not strong enough. It helped me to feel like myself again, to put things in perspective, that this is my life, and I'm taking control of it by any means necessary! If that means going to a therapist or taking medication, so be it. This is my life, and I plan to start living like it is MY life, not my friends, family, or anyone else's life but mine. This time, it's personal. I owe it not only to my children, but to myself, and I have learned it is ok to feel like this. I owe it to myself. I feel stronger today than I did last year all because, girl, I took my medication.

Depression! Why Does It Still Hurt?

Sonya Lyons

Depression affects people because they get so wrapped up with the process of living day to day that they begin to lose interest in their life and what they are going through, so they neglect God's word. They feel the weight of serving God because the joy is gone, and they are left with the dull mechanics of living. Like a dark tunnel with no exit.

I went through a divorce because I had to free myself from that bondage for my sanity and pray for God's forgiveness. I honestly felt God frowned on divorce, and I would be punished for leaving. I went into a deep, deep depression that lasted for about two years. God allowed me to become broken before him so that I could hear him. I wasn't happy in it, and I wasn't happy out of it. I didn't want to be bothered with anyone. I would isolate myself from family and friends, and I had to start all over. It truly felt like a death, and it was; it was the death of a relationship that was vowed before God that I would be in until death did we part.

God had to mold me and reshape me to get me back on the right track toward my destiny since the enemy pulled me off course. My transition was not personal; it was my testimony so I would be able to help someone else while giving God the Glory for overcoming it. God gives us the freedom of choice, and sometimes, we get deceived and choose the other path that God has not chosen for us, so he will allow us to go down that path, and when we hit that barrier in the road, he waits for us to cry out to him before he takes control again.

King Saul was affected by depression. He called for David to play and sing the anointed Psalms. Of all cities in the world, none has been so frequently attacked like Jerusalem. Why is it so? It is because the place has a prophetic destiny. So, as a child of God, in case you are seriously under attack or you are wondering why you are sweating and struggling, it means that there is something in your destiny that the enemy does not want to happen:

Isaiah 59:19 – So shall they fear the name of the LORD from the west, and his glory from the rising of the sun. When the enemy shall come in like a flood, the Spirit of the LORD shall lift up a standard against him.

You can give in to depression or resist it. When you offer yourselves to someone/something as obedient slaves, you are slaves of the one you obey— whether you are slaves to sin, which leads to death, or to obedience, which leads to righteousness:

Romans 6:16 – Know ye not, that to whom ye yield yourselves servants to obey, his servants ye are to whom ye obey; whether of sin unto death, or of obedience unto righteousness?

Don't give in to the spirit of heaviness—but use the word of God like a sword. When the devil says you're no good, remind him of:

2 Corinthians 5:17 – Therefore if any man be in Christ, he is a new creature: old things are passed away; behold, all things are become new.

When the devil says you're not saved, just tell him I know I'm saved because I was there when it happened. When the devil says to worry, just remind him that God said don't worry about anything. When the devil says be sick, just tell him by his stripes I am healed. When he says be afraid, remind him God said my peace I give to you. When he says be defeated, say we are more than conquerors through him that loved us.

We are all going to face adversity. Even Paul did. A person comes under attack because the enemy wants to conquer him, the enemy wants to suppress him, the enemy wants to contend with his destiny, his existence is threatening the existence of another person or his destiny is an eagle destiny.

We all experience pain in life. Heartache, loss, disappointment. Suffering is a part of being human. When you're in the depths of it, it can be hard to see how you can ever recover from your deep pain. The idea that you might one day be grateful for your disappointment and hurt seems unthinkable. Yet, we always have a choice. Even in our pain, we have a choice to make. We get to decide whether we will take the opportunity and grow, or whether we will let it consume us.

I by no means intend to make this seem simple; it may be the hardest thing you will ever do. But your pain may also be the thing that pushes you toward your greatest personal breakthroughs. It is our hurt that can crack us open and let the light in. It is your pain that can help move us toward living a more deeply fulfilling life. There is a psychological idea known as Post-Traumatic Growth. We are all familiar with its cousin, post-traumatic stress. Post-traumatic growth isn't discussed as frequently, but it is the concept that explains how many of us take our pain and use it as the energy to grow psychologically.

Post-traumatic growth is not about returning to the same life as it was previously experienced before a period of traumatic suffering; but rather it is about undergoing significant 'life-changing' psychological shifts in thinking and relating to the world that contribute to a personal process of change that is deeply meaningful. We need to get in touch with our emotions and be willing to feel them. To understand why we hurt, we must dip deep into where the pain is stemming from. It is easy to say we are hurt because of heartbreak, but the question is, what part of the heartbreak is really causing us the pain? Is it that we feel like a failure? That we are grieving for a future that no longer exists? Or that we don't feel worthy of love? We need to express our emotions and work through them until we can find their root cause. Self-reflection and personal understanding are prerequisites to deeper psychological growth. To grow from a painful experience, we need to focus our minds on looking for the lesson. This is one way of choosing to have a growth-mindset. No matter what the situation, we will be able to uncover a lesson if we look hard enough. If you have been faced with an illness, perhaps it can teach you what you need to prioritize in life. If you are recovering from heartbreak, perhaps it can highlight your need to respect yourself more so that you are not prone to letting other people disrespect you.

Looking for the lesson is about taking your power back. You can't wallow indefinitely in the pain if you are to step up and grow. Once you've identified the root cause of your hurt, you have the power to look for what you can learn from the situation. Once you can acknowledge what your current situation might have to teach you, you need to resolve to change. Real growth must be followed by action. You have to do things differently. This is where your pain can truly turn into your greatest power.

It may be that you re-prioritize how you live your life so that the things that really matter to you play a bigger part. Or you may try to focus on truly deep-down loving yourself before you begin to look for another romantic partner. Your actions will always be so personal to you.

Real growth comes from a willingness to change. You need to do things differently and use your pain as the thing that leads you on your path to growth. You can turn your pain into power. If you are willing to work out where the pain stems from, recognize there is a lesson to be learned, and turn your new knowledge into action, you will come through the suffering a brighter and stronger person. So why does it still hurt? It still hurts as a reminder to take that pain and convert it into something positive. It's also a reminder of where God has bought you from. Your purpose is in your pain. I now speak all over the country to men and women about relationships and how important it is to have God in our lives and in our relationships. I cater to the women because I was one of those who sacrificed so much just to be in a relationship. I have a bestselling book out called *Why Am I Not Married? Independence, Is It A Blessing Or Curse?* that talks about being single, being married, being divorced, being depressed, and not feeling accepted with low self-esteem. Not that I'm an expert, but there was a purpose in my pain, and I can't help anyone if I had not walked through it myself...

Now, it's my hope that you will get up and win, girl!

Never Quit

Maggie Vincent

Sometimes when you try to improve your life, obstacles will stand in your way at the worse possible moment to deter you from realizing the goals you have set for yourself. You must be vigilant and stand strong to face whatever comes your way. Somehow, something within you is always ready to convince you that it is so much easier to get comfortable where you are than to press on to change your current situation. Even though you are sick and tired of your present condition, you may give in to the force of getting comfortable and fail to take action to change what you cannot stomach. The great news is you really do not have to accept what you do not like in your life; you have a choice to change it to whatever your heart desires. You just need to know how to equip yourself to overcome the voice that is whispering to you it is not possible. I will share with you how I had overcome my own fear of reaching the next level in my life during my divorce. I will also prove to you that it's always possible for you to reach the next level in whatever goals you have set for yourself.

Girl, Get Up and Win

Back in 2000, I started working at a hospital as a nursing assistant; a nursing assistant works alongside a registered nurse to assist patients with performing their personal care, such as bathing, feeding, measuring a simple blood pressure or temperature, and reporting the findings to the registered nurse. As I was functioning in that role for about one year, I became displeased with my role. I wanted to be more. My choices were limited; I was not able to attend college yet because I was not an American citizen. I migrated here back in 1992 from my native land, and the process of obtaining a residential status was the longest for me. I completed my last year of high school in the USA, and I attempted to go to college; however, I was being charged out-of-state tuition fees, yet my monthly wages were less than the fund that was required to pay for one class.

In addition to that, I still had to pay for my living expenses. I was not aware of any resources for non-residents. I waited nine years to be granted a residential status; by 2001, I went to college; however, I was married with three children ranging from ages of three to five years old while working full-time and sometimes extra time at the hospital. Despite all my challenges, which were not limited to dealing with hostility from my ex who was not thrilled with my idea of seeking further education, the one person I desperately sought approval from; having him abruptly quit his job while I was in my first semester of nursing, with zero consideration of what might happen to our mortgage and our three children; and the constant "you think you're better than me"—one day I told him I would not quit school no matter what he threw at me.

I walked my path through my trials, and I earned an associate degree within three years, one year of fifteen required classes and two years of the nursing program. I graduated with honor and was offered a scholarship to proceed with further studies, but I wanted to be fair. I chose to work to give my ex-husband a chance to study while I paid the bills in the hope that he would study something worthy of earning enough money to alleviate my burden of working sixty hours per week while I still continued to take at least one class per semester to complete my general study at the state college. My ex went for a fifteen-month program for license practical nurse; he completed the program, but never committed to obtain the state license to practice even though he had a loan. I was back in the same corner of working more to pay for most of the bills. I decided to go back to school full-time, attending classes toward a different major, a pharmacist or a nurse anesthetist. Although I completed my general degree and had an associate degree in nursing, I did not have a bachelor's degree because I was afraid of writing long papers. I ended up taking more science classes toward those two majors because I was desperate to find a better way to make more money in less working days. My life was consumed by work outside my home and at home. I was playing too many roles simultaneously: a mother, a wife, and a worker of two different jobs. As for myself, I did not exist. Meanwhile, my marriage was getting worse until my ex-husband left the house. My children, two daughters and one son were between teens and pre-teens: fourteen, thirteen, and twelve.

Oh my God! I remember that day when I entered my door from work; my oldest daughter told me her dad had moved out and left the key with her. Oh, the fear that spread through all my bones like an electrical current hit a pond. I did not know what to do; that night, I sat in my room and told myself I had a decision to make. I decided to leave my regular job which consisted of four to five 12-hour shifts per week, from 7 a.m. to 7:30 p.m. I left my job within one month and went to work for another company Monday through Friday from 8 a.m. to 4 p.m. That schedule allowed me time to drop the kids to school, pick them up in the afternoon, and be present at home with them. Sometimes, you can be in the house, but not present. Being present means I had to be available to listen to their concerns after school, attempt to dig up thoughts they were suppressing during the tough moments, as well as taking them to some sort of therapy. After a long day with my children, then came the nights where I fell asleep on wet pillows from my own tears. When I examined my kids, I also realized I had to make a second decision. I could continue to pursue my goal to become a nurse anesthetist or a pharmacist, or I could take the time to ensure proper structure of my children so they, too, could have a better life, or I could neglect them and just see to myself.

I chose to free up time to care for my children. I had so many class credits in college, but I did not have a bachelor's degree in any major; most employers were already demanding a bachelor's degree in nursing. I had to face my fear of not wanting to write. I visited the university to gather information about what I had postponed for so long due to my fear of writing. I looked at myself in the mirror for over a month, and at each occasion when I was feeling less of myself, I exclaim to myself, "It is true English is not your primary language, but you can still do well; you will just have to follow the rules of the language and apply them just like you have in everything else you have already succeeded in." Then, I submitted my application to get my bachelor's degree in the science of nursing.

Sometimes, you must use any means possible to conquer that voice that is telling you that you can't. Somehow, I told myself I could not write even though I only earned one C throughout college; everything else were A's and B's. If you are not from the United States, a C grade is equivalent to 70-79%, a B is 80-89%, and an A is 90-100%. Now, I cannot even remember what persuaded me to believe that I could not write. I no longer use the word "cannot." One thing I chose not do was to stop taking classes during my divorce. Although it was extremely difficult to keep a straight face at work while dealing with the emotional cascade during separation then divorce proceeding, I convinced myself I had to keep pushing. I just sensed if I had stopped at any time during my difficult moment that I would not have gone back; I just could not allow myself to be told I could not provide for my children and myself simply because I held on to a belief that was completely false. It was not an easy balance to maintain work, school, care for teenagers, and divorce. There were times I was crying in room while writing my papers; my papers were often marked with tear drops, but I had refused to quit. I was not familiar with typing on the computer. I would handwrite the whole paper, then

127

type it. With time, I got better to the point that one of my professors wrote one of my long papers that I was afraid to write, "You write so well. You should be a writer." Oh wow! How did I go from doubting myself to getting such a compliment? It's called determination, perseverance, and having a strong "why." It took me six months longer, but in two and half years, I walked the stage to get my diploma.

This success also came from releasing my own limiting belief. I share my story with you not to brag about myself or my accomplishment; my intent is far from those things. By now I understand, it is not necessary for me to seek anyone's approval of who I am, but I share it to inspire you to start taking actions on what you have envisioned for so long, but you cannot seem to even start. I share my story with you so that you will know you have what it takes, you are able to do anything you want; it does not matter what challenges lie ahead, if you can escape your own self, persevere, and focus on the reasons you are aiming for that goal, you will be able to achieve it. You will encounter others who will enumerate multiple reasons why you will fail; you will just have to develop a death ear to them. Your biggest fight is yourself. Make the choice to conquer it to get to your finish line.

How to Move Out of the Darkness and into the Light

Kendra Kay Woods, MBA

I didn't know it then, but my life started going downhill in 2012. There I was looking like I had it all together. I was a master at putting on a smile and making people think that I was all good and all together. I did all the things that I thought I was supposed to do in my life in order to be happy. I graduated high school like my parents told me to. I went on to attend college, and not only did I get one degree, but I got two degrees. I met an amazing man, got married, bought a house, and gave birth to my beautiful daughter. I was checking off all the boxes because I had a perception that by checking off these boxes my life would be the happily ever after fairy tale. After I graduated with my master's degree, I landed an amazing job that provided me with the status and income that I believed I needed to be happy and fulfilled. However, every day I woke up and went through the motions of living my life, but something was not quite right at all. Here I was with so much to be grateful for, yet I had such a heavy feeling on the inside of me. I was fighting a losing battle within myself because my mindset, self-worth, and confidence were literally put to the test daily. I was so fragile mentally and emotionally, and it began to show up in ways that I couldn't control.

I began to experience a heavy feeling of sadness, depression, anxiety, stress, fatigue, and so much inner tension that I felt like a ball of nerves on most days. Yet there I was, putting on my makeup every day, styling my hair just right, putting on my well-fitted suit, slipping on my beautiful heels, and grabbing my designer handbag and heading in to work every day. I looked so polished, put together, and professional on the outside, yet on the inside, I was literally a train wreck waiting to happen. I wasn't happy by any means, but I was too afraid to admit this to myself. I couldn't understand how I could have so much outward success in my life and still feel such a deep sinking feeling within myself. I kept thinking that one day I would snap out of it, and things were going to get better. I found myself not showing up in a healthy way with my husband or with my daughter. I had very little patience with my daughter who at the peak of my depressed state was 3 years old. I was holding so much resentment and anger toward my husband, and I would simply shut down anytime there was any tension between him and me. I knew this wasn't the way I wanted to live, and I knew this wasn't the way I wanted to show up for my life, so what did I do? I proceeded to beat myself up and make myself wrong for everything that was happening in my life. I was so hard on myself, and I couldn't figure out why I couldn't just snap out of this dark place I was in.

As a result of me being in what I call The Black Hole, I experienced severe bouts of anxiety, weight gain, severe fatigue, and of course depression. I began to isolate myself because I believed no one would understand what I was going through. I believed that people would think I was weak and couldn't handle life if I spoke up about what I was going through. So instead of giving myself permission to be supported, I chose to spend countless hours on my sofa every night numbing myself out with TV and snacks, hence the reason why I put on extra weight. I did not like the woman that I saw in the mirror, I didn't recognize her. The joy and laughter had left my life, and it was like a shell of myself was just walking around every day going through the motions. This way of being went on for a couple of years, and then one day my world came crashing down all around me. One day while at work, I showed up with my beautiful mask on that said to the world I had all my stuff together, and with no warning at all, I had a full blown anxiety episode in one of the medical offices that I was managing at the time. I ended up lying on an exam table with my doctors (whose practice I was managing) and staff standing over me, checking my vitals to be sure that I was okay and wasn't having some kind of cardiac episode. I was utterly embarrassed and wanted to hide under a rock. It took two of my staff to help me get back to my office where I literally lost my composure and cried my eyeballs out. I was mortified and couldn't believe that I was so exposed and vulnerable. My husband had to come pick me up from work, and for the rest of the day and into the next day, I slept.

In the days that followed, I realized that I needed to make a change because I could no longer go on living my life in such a fragile state. I knew that if I kept going down the path I was headed I wouldn't be around to enjoy my family. As I lay in bed wide awake in the wee hours of the morning one day, I made a silent promise to myself that I was going to get my life together. I promised myself that I would have a life where I was happy and full of joy. So, in April of 2016, I took back control over my life and started pulling myself out of the pit of the black hole that I found myself in. Looking back at that time, I now realize that I wasn't alone in what I was going through because there are many women in this world who are suffering in silence right now, afraid to say anything for fear of judgment or criticism. This woman may be you reading this book right now, and if so, I want you to know that you are not alone. I want you to know that you can pull yourself up and win at life. You do have the capacity to move through the depression, the anxiety, and any other heavy feelings from within you may be facing. What I have learned through my own personal journey is that we are our own hero. You cannot put the responsibility on someone else to make you feel better. You have been given the power to do that for yourself.

I knew at the time and deeply believed that I would be able to heal myself, and that is exactly what I did. I decided that I was going to take back my power, and I started brainstorming ways in which I could get myself together and feeling whole again. I remember thinking of things that made me feel good. I remember thinking that for this to work, I would need to ensure that I made myself number one priority and that I did what I needed for my soul first thing in the morning before anyone could tap into my energy. It was time for me to start saying yes to myself and my dreams. Now this may seem a little extreme to some, but when you are desperate and at rock bottom, you will do whatever you need to do to get yourself together again. I decided that before anyone had the opportunity to request anything from me, I would spend time each morning pouring into myself first. I committed to waking each day between 3:30 a.m. and 4 a.m. to spend time working on me, and I want to share with you what I did to pull myself out of the darkness.

I decided that I would dedicate one hour each morning filling up my soul before I gave anything to anyone else. I created what I call my Sacred Morning Manifestation Routine. Each morning, for that one hour, I did the following activities–read an uplifting personal development book, pray, visualize, exercise, meditate, journal, and read affirmations.

Over the course of the months that followed, I noticed that I began feeling lighter, and there was hope back in my life again. I realized that it was important for me to get crystal clear on what I wanted from my life because much of the darkness I was facing came from me trying to mold my life based on the expectations of others. You have to live your life for you and always make you your number one priority. Often when you experience heavy feelings of depression or anxiety, it's because you are pushing down the desires of your soul. So now is the time for you to start saying yes to your life and to your dreams. I can honestly say that because of my commitment to my Sacred Morning Manifestation routine, I was able

133

to turn my life around. Blessings began to show up in my life. I was actually let go from my job during my transition of taking back my life, and it was the best thing that could have happened to me. That allowed me to really create my life deliberately, and now I get the pleasure of being CEO of my life coaching practice, being home with my daughter, more in love with my husband than ever before, 20 pounds lighter, a deep soulful love for myself, and an inner world full of peace and joy. It is possible for you to win in your life; it just takes you putting your foot down, taking back your power, and deliberately creating the life you desire to live. I believe in you.

Dismantling Brokenness and Building Self-Esteem

Girl, Get Up and Win

All the Darkness in the World Cannot Blow Out My Candle

Carol Boss

What is grief? A deep sorrow that is related to someone's death...or loss.

My name is Carol, and within thirty days, I had signed my dissolution of marriage after 17 years; a few weeks later, I lost my father and then my mother. They were 3,000 miles away from each other, in California and North Carolina, when this happened. They both had strokes, went into ICU, and passed two weeks later, and both were buried in the same week in January 2019. As this was happening, I was no longer working and stood by their side.

I screamed, cried, vomited, and was sick to my stomach. A flood of emotions were at an all-time high. My heart felt broken in a million pieces. A miracle of catastrophic circumstances led to not working and the loss of the three loves of my life.

While my mom was in ICU, I fell to my knees and got into deep meditation where there were no more tears—just a sense of calmness.

Then my heart began to speak. I realized in that moment I had experienced the greatest unconditional love from my mother that most will never experience. I had expressed my deepest concerns, revealed my true self, and was accepted no matter what. I was fully guided with the intentions from her to see me at my best with joy and being fulfilled. An abundance of gratitude had filled me in that moment.

I knew then that this experience was for my highest good and that no one knew ME except my mother. These thoughts of uncertainty and unfulfillment was how I had been living, and I was not in my truth.

I began to look over her life. As she departed this life at 64, was she whole, having lived a fulfilled life? The answer was yes because she lived in the moment and did whatever she wanted to do, met no stranger, and lived her truth. Everyone KNEW her.

I began to feel empowered; my mind became vibrant, and for the first time, I was not just open to fulfillment in my life—I was willing to take action.

I wondered if I was going to allow this event to define me, allow my current circumstances of not working a job, a dissolution signed , and the death of both my parents all in 30 days be the reason to spiral down into an emotional state of being with no drive, no purpose in life, no dreams to catch, no message to convey to the world, nothing to accomplish, nothing to stand for, and no loving, spiritually connected relationship to experience either.

I immediately began to visualize the story I created thus far in my life, acknowledged it, accepted it and what I contributed. I am where I am now because I allowed myself to show up that way, and I was committed to it regardless if it was serving me well or not.

For the first time, I no longer wanted to continue the story, or turn the page, or even start a new chapter. I set that bitch, the whole book, on fire and started a whole new book. I am creating a new story of experiences of inspiration, connections, spiritual growth, contribution, romance, love, and self-wealth.

Pain and loss have illuminated my glow, my light; ignited my fire for love to rest with in me, an unexplainable gift of gratitude in abundance; expedited my growth in emotional intelligence; tapped in to a spiritual connection directly to the source, a self-worth approval well that is profound; embraced my intuitive empathic gift; opened my heart to a loving undeniable understanding of compassion; and opened my mind to manifest self-wealth in my life and others.

My father, mother, both my grandfathers, and many family members were all entrepreneurs and inventors. I have the opportunity to continue my entrepreneurship and create the liberty and life I truly deserve. I am excited to see the manifestations I create by this December 2019.

I share this because I have the choice of free will and so do you. Divorce, death of family, and loss of work all at the same time have been my greatest challenges; however; they have been my greatest lessons in life.

And your challenges can become *your* greatest lessons, too, and lead you to success beyond your imagination.

To Overcome Brokenness

Noreen N.
Henry

What is brokenness? Why talk about the topic of brokenness now?

Brokenness is a topic that I haven't seen addressed. You never hear anyone talk about it. Yet, it is at the root of many issues. So, this is a timely topic that needs exposure in order for the brokenness in us not only to heal, but to be prevented in the first place, and this will be accomplished as we gain the correct knowledge.

Definition of brokenness: violently separated into parts. Shattered. Violated. Damaged or altered. Not properly working, not functioning properly, out of working order. Irregular, interrupted, or full of obstacles. Not kept or honored. Crushed. Sorrowful. Not complete or full. Disunited. Reduced to fragments. Covered by clouds.

As you can see from the definitions of brokenness, being broken is terribly negative. Logically, it produces negativity in our lives, especially when it's not dealt with in the right way. And I know from experience that it will continue to get worse until it is dealt with properly. I saw this in my life, and I see it in others' lives.

Let's take a good look at the meanings of brokenness, violently separated into parts, damaged, crushed, reduced to fragments, shattered, etc. Let's see what shattered means. Shattered means broken into many pieces. My Lord! I was shattered, I was broken into many pieces. Layers and layers of brokenness. But, I am happy to say each layer of brokenness has been removed one by one. Even though there is still more work to be done, I've come a long way; it is a lifelong process.

It was many years of brokenness. Each layer is dealt with individually until I overcome it, and then the next area is revealed to me in order to work on it. For instance, the next area for me is working on food addiction. This is how dealing with the layers of brokenness has worked for me.

Another area of brokenness is not being free to be your true self the way you were created to be. We were designed to be free and whole, not burdened down with so many issues of hurt and pain.

It is sad to see so many people walking around broken. It has horrible repercussions, even more issues. When children commit suicide, it's because they are broken. When adolescents do shootings at schools, it's because they are broken. When people end up in mental institutions, it's because they are broken. Adults that commit suicide are broken. People that are depressed are broken. When people self-mutilate, it is because of brokenness. When people have addictions, it's due to brokenness. The list can go on and on and on. We, as a society, need to wake up and realize that brokenness is real and that we can, and must, be healed from it. Furthermore, with the right knowledge, we can help to prevent it.

I believe brokenness starts in childhood. For me, it started at birth when I was told I was ugly. The words were not meant, but it was a negative start to my life. Growing up and even into my adult years, I thought I was ugly. I also thought I was fat.

I was broken for many years, but I didn't know it. I am the type of person who keeps moving forward, accomplishing great things, e.g. becoming an ordained minister. But, I didn't recognize I was broken and needed to be healed internally, at the heart level.

Quite frankly, I don't remember how I knew I was broken, but there was a time in my life when I started saying my heart is hard. I could feel it, and I wanted relief from that. That's when I knew I needed inner healing. [Note: God always leads us to what we need. The steps of a good man/woman are ordered by the Lord, Psalm 37:23.] Several years ago, when I told someone my heart was hard, the response was a shocked look because based on the kind of person I am, how could I have a hard heart? When I said it to my sister, she started singing the song "Heart Made of Stone." We laughed about it even though it was serious. This was one of the layers of brokenness I've healed. Today, my heart isn't hard anymore.

When I went through the terrible divorce from my children's father, I didn't cry throughout the whole ordeal. I was just functioning. Over the years, there were many things that I should have cried about, but I never did. This was due to my heart being hard because of the brokenness.

An area of brokenness came from leaving my home town of London, England, and migrating to the United States of America. Even though my parents told us there were more opportunities over here, it didn't stop the brokenness. We were torn away from all we knew and went to a strange land. The crying that took place when we were leaving our family and friends at the airport was unreal. I realized many, many years later how deeply that move affected me. That has been another layer of brokenness to deal with. This shows me that this was a layer of brokenness that was buried, then eventually surfaced, I believe, as I've been working on my inner healing.

I was broken due to being in an unhappy relationship, that was another layer, in fact layers, and trying to make it work for years. I had become angry and was always yelling. My children grew up with me in that way. When my son was a teenager, he told me that when Mum is happy, everyone is happy. Then the last straw was finding out about the adultery. I felt ashamed and embarrassed to know that someone who said they loved you could do this to you. [Note: being embarrassed and ashamed adds more layers of brokenness.] And that wasn't all, I was emotionally abused for years, and the thing is, I allowed it. The Bible says we perish for lack of knowledge, and we really do (Hosea 4:6). I allowed it because I thought things would get better, so I stayed in the abusive relationship. What's the saying? Insanity is doing the same thing over and over and expecting different results ☺.

When the unhappy relationship ended in divorce, it was such a confusing time in my life. I was confused for a long time, so imagine that effect on my children watching me. It didn't help my children. We were all hurt and all broken. I wasn't valued or thought well of, and this added layers of brokenness. I had developed food addiction, which was a result of rejection, and that too is brokenness. Any kind of addiction is due to brokenness.

For years, I suffered being broken, and like I already mentioned, I didn't know I was broken. This is another issue to deal with. Many don't realize they are broken and think they are fine. Seeing choices that people make tells me that they are broken. I want to help them so badly, but they have to want it. First, they have to recognize that something is wrong and that they need help. There was a time I started saying I need help. I had recognized that I needed help. I wanted change.

I got to the point of enough is enough. I wanted a better life. It's like I always knew there was better and more to life. I just didn't know how to get it.

Now, I always work on my inner self, and that has helped me tremendously. I look within and examine myself and continuously work on me. I also have God in my life, and that's the biggest help.

Brokenness can come about in any relationship. Relationships between parents and children, between boss and employee, etc. Yes, even work life can add layers of brokenness to you.

I see so many broken people who with the right help and commitment to doing the work will be just fine. I can attest to this because I am proof of it. There will always be issues, but compared to before, I am doing great. Things will come up, but I'm not broken anymore.

How I overcame the brokenness

I didn't get healed overnight. It has taken years of working on myself.

After my former husband walked away from my children and me, I began working on myself much more. The first thing I did was order the emotional healing package by Joyce Meyer. I did a lot of reading. Whatever was going on, I would look for books that dealt with it.

What sped up the healing was when I started inner healing coaching and went on from there to a healing retreat. All of this has helped with getting past the brokenness. It was at the healing retreat that I was delivered from the hard heart. In fact, previous to this, I had volunteered at an event and during one of the exercises, I started bawling and bawling. A bunch of people surrounded me, held me, and said positive things to me. I couldn't believe that happened, especially since I was a volunteer, but it was needed; it was time to have more inner healing. In another session I had taken, the exercise was to change the negative words of no value to "I am more than good enough," and I still say this today.

It's not an easy process to get through the brokenness because you have to bring up the hurt in order to deal with the issues. But believe me, it is worth it. I can say I am free. I have been liberated and free to be me. Free to thrive and help others do the same.

What the enemy means for harm, the Lord turns around for the good to help many (Genesis 50:50), and I'm a perfect example of that. I learned to live victoriously and learned that there is always hope. I also changed my family's legacy and my own legacy. I now teach others the tools to live a victorious life, and there are many aspects to victorious living as I mention in my multiple #1 bestseller, *Victorious Living: Guide to a Happier Life*.

There is always a solution. You may not want to hear it, but when you implement the solution, you are much better off. For example, my solution was to escape the bondage of the relationship I was in, and since then, I've gotten back to how I was before: happy. In fact, I say I am back to myself, and this is a better version of me.

I am so glad that I forgive and I didn't get bitter or resentful in spite all that has happened to me. I am also glad that I work on myself continually.

You, too, can overcome the brokenness; I testify to that.

Finally Forgiven and Free

Linda S. Husser

Without a doubt, having four abortions was my biggest hurdle to overcome. I even thought that God was punishing me with herpes for having terminated so many pregnancies. Surely, *He* wasn't going to let me off scot-free after doing the unthinkable four times, right? I even would have nightmares of hearing my babies cry. My mind was playing tricks on me, and I knew that I had to find a way to forgive myself for the traumatic life choices that I had made if ever I was to have a chance of living a life of purpose, passion, and possibilities.

You are probably asking yourself why did I have so many abortions, right? Because I was irresponsible, lonely, full of self-doubt, and incredibly low self-esteem. I was having unprotected sex with numerous men because I was looking for acceptance and love. It never even dawned on me to have my partners wear a condom. I was playing Russian roulette with my life and could have contracted HIV. And while HIV today is quite manageable, in the '80s it wasn't. I thank God I am still here.

I had my first abortion when I was 18 and my last one at 29. I had two of them in California, one in London, England, and another in San Antonio, Texas. Now that I have worked on my self-esteem, had therapy, and engaged in regular spiritual practices, it seems surreal that I was so out of alignment with my true magnificence. When I got pregnant for the fourth time, I was crushed. After I peed on the EPT strip, I prayed a mighty prayer. I told God that if He would just let me not be pregnant, I would straighten up and fly right. No more casual sex and multiple partners. But then, I watched in utter horror as the strip turned pink. Oh no. Frantically, I grabbed another one, peed on it, and watched the strip again. There had to be something wrong with it! Why was it turning pink?! It felt like my soul was smothered, and my light would never shine again.

How did I get here? What was I going to do? The thought of another procedure sickened me, and for a whole week, I just laid in bed feeling sorry for myself. Should I call the baby's father and talk to him about it? Even though we were casual sex partners, maybe it could turn into a real relationship for the sake of the child. Who was I kidding? We didn't have a *relationship* and simply got together to have sex. So many times I wanted to tell him that I was pregnant, but I just couldn't. I just abruptly stopped having sex with him and avoiding places where he frequented.

After a week of beating myself up, I decided not to have the baby. I toyed with the idea of keeping it for a split second. Then I punked out. My embarrassment and shame for getting pregnant was stronger than my spiritual beliefs. It washed over me like a waterfall, and I felt like I was drowning in it. The saddest part about this was that I couldn't tell anyone how I was feeling. This was a secret I was pretty sure I would take to my grave. There was NO way I was going to tell ANYONE that I was getting ready to have abortion number *four*.

When I think about it now, I realize just how disconnected I was from God even though I asked to be forgiven. I had some nerve calling out to God when I was going to have an abortion. But I called Him anyway. He was supposed to be our comforter even when we did bad things. At least that was how I saw it. Unfortunately, I didn't see He would also have given me the strength to give birth and care for the baby as a single mother. It's not like I would have been the only one in the world who got pregnant out of wedlock.

After the procedure, I went into a funk. Not a full blown depression, but close. I wasn't sleeping properly, lost weight, and was smoking a pack and a half of Newport Kings a day. I was a hot mess! This was no way to live. It was at this point that I had to take a long hard look at myself and what I was doing. It was NOT ok to use abortion as a birth control method. It was not ok to devalue myself. I had to stop having meaningless sex with random men and take a look at the woman in the mirror. I was asking her to make a change.

My journey back to me began with attending a forgiveness seminar given at my local community college. While I was working on my relationship with God, I still wanted a support group and some practical tools and tips on how to forgive myself for my multiple abortions. This was the best decision I could have ever made! I learned while I couldn't change my choices, I could change *my response to my choices*. This was life-changing and set me free!

The three points that our teacher gave us to memorize and recite every morning upon waking were:

- If you don't let go of the pain, it won't let go of you!
- No pity parties
- Don't erase your story, embrace your story!

Sounds pretty simple, doesn't it? That's why it works! We complicate things way too much. Our minds are the soil in which our thoughts live. We must plant positive affirmations and allow good thoughts to germinate and grow.

It feels good to be in a much different place today! The decisions that I made when I had low self-esteem and an inferiority complex are hard to fathom now that I honor and love myself. I am excited to finally say that I have learned to manage my imperfections. And it feels really good to no longer be hiding in the shadows. It was time to come out and face the music. I needed to take back my power that I had willingly handed over to my abortions. I know how to empower, love, and forgive myself now. These three principles are paramount to having a life of joy, peace, love, and hope.

The Death of My Spirit

Kimmoly K. LaBoo

(Journal entries by Kimmoly K. LaBoo)

6/12/2012 – For the past week I have been, in my definition, unproductive. I'm not really sure what this season is that I am going through. I have a million things to do, yet I feel as though I have no direction.

6/20/2012 – Frustrated – I still haven't figured out what this temporary halt is about. I still haven't been able to shake it. What I do know is it is frustrating the heck out of me. I see the days passing me by, and I just sit and stare and watch them go. What in the heck is that? I feel like I am just waiting for something. That is not like me at all. I am the one who normally makes things happen. I'm drawing blanks right now. It is even a struggle to find the words to pen tonight.

…Lord, I need your help with this one. I'm calling on you! Standing on Proverbs 3:5. Amen.

9/21/2012 – *It's been three months since I've written. Amazingly enough, it's almost as if time is standing still. I'm still feeling stagnant. I know there is something I am supposed to be learning right now in this season. There is a part of me that feels somewhat broken. I'm trying desperately to recover. When someone pushes you and pushes you to the breaking point, eventually it happens no matter how strong you are. No one can endure continual beating of the soul, mind, spirit, and self-esteem without breaking at some point. I hate the fact that I broke. I don't know if it is pride, anger, or remnants of a broken heart. I don't understand why people hurt those who are closest to them. I guess it is all a part of the mask. No way would you treat an outsider with utter disdain; that would blow your cover and allow people to see the real you, and then where would you be? I am your safe place, yet you abuse me with your words. I have faced the hard reality that I need to "redefine" my definition of abuse. For years, I have said things like, "As long as he doesn't hit me, I'm good." I realize now that words cut just as deep as a knife and wound as deep as a bullet. I am no longer blinded by the false reality that it takes a punch, slap, or kick to constitute abuse. I demand more, I expect more, I am more, and I have resolved within myself that if I have to walk away in order to have it, I will. I am not enslaved by material things. I have never been nor will I ever be. I love me.*

Now that I have that off my chest, I say, Lord, I thank you for never leaving me, despite my shortcomings during this difficult season in my life. I know that you know at times I have been upset with you. I have been feeling angry because I couldn't understand why you would have him take me to the breaking point when I have tried so hard to be strong and uphold your standard. I realize now that you were letting me see that I didn't always have to be that (strong). I recognize that only your grace has carried me though. It's because of you that I am not crazy, in jail, or just plain old bitter. I know he had to fall, I just didn't expect that he would actually take me with him, but through it all you are still faithful. I am grateful.

In 2013, I decided to go on a 12-month Personal Courage journey. For the entire year, I did something new every month. I went skydiving to prove to myself that I was fearless. I learned to swim to prove to myself I was courageous. I travelled to Ghana, West Africa, to prove to myself that my voice still mattered and had value. I walked on my treadmill for 31 days straight to prove to myself I had the willpower to make things happen. I volunteered to feed the homeless to demonstrate that I still had compassion. I got braces on my teeth because I knew soon, I was going to have something to smile about again. It was my year of rediscovering me.

5/3/2014 – Today, I am sitting in my office trying to figure out what my next step in this journey called life will be. There is so much going on. I'm unsure about my marriage. Well, actually, that's not true. I know exactly where I am and exactly where I need to be and what I need to do. The challenge is in the execution of it all. Sometimes, it is hard to stop the train to let passengers off when you're travelling at an accelerated speed. However, I know it's time to slow it down to allow someone and somethings to step off. I'm gaining my courage and asking for the help I need in order to make it happen.

12/31/2014 – We are just moments away from 2015. This has been a very challenging and rewarding year all at the same time. From the moment I decided to choose me, things have gotten a lot better. Walking away from a destructive marriage was the best thing for me and my children. Things had gotten so bad that it wasn't really difficult to walk away. June was the beginning of me reclaiming my inner peace and joy. I made a choice not to accept the bad behavior that was stripping me of my internal peace and joy. I could no longer live a life that didn't line up with my message and my beliefs. No more name calling, no more yelling of obscenities, no more bullying and mind games. Enough is enough. I'm done. The great thing is I'm not angry and I am not bitter. I am grateful to God for that.

I pray that he finds internal peace, joy, and healing at some point. I just can't continue to be a verbal punching bag, feeling the full impact of his vulgar words as if they were being delivered as a physical punch. Those days are over for good. I Choose Me!

I thank you Lord, for keeping my mind in perfect peace. I thank and praise your Holy name. You are my joy, my strength, my rock, my protector, my redeemer. Amen!

I didn't realize the hit that my spirit was taking while I was in the destruction. When I broke free, I discovered I had been walking wounded. It took years to recover. While I was in my season of despair, my constant prayer was, Lord, give me peace, I just want peace.

Two years after I walked away, God blessed me with the opportunity of a lifetime. I now live on the beautiful island of Oahu, Hawai'i. There is peace and healing here. It was the perfect place for my spirit to recover. Today, I live a happy, vibrant, and blessed life. God answered my prayer after "I chose me!"

If ever you find yourself in a situation that is depleting your spirit, choose you!

People Pleasers

Cheryl Peavy

What does it mean to break someone's spirit? When a person's spirit is broken, they often feel they aren't deserving of joy, or they may have even totally lost all hope or desire for happiness; it's a feeling of total emotional defeat. This is what I got off the Internet. I don't want to quote this, but I had a broken spirit that turned me into a people pleaser.

Breaking the spirit of people, I am sad to say, is an accepted method of control in our society. It is done in some cases as part of a regimen of discipline, by others unwittingly as they are not aware of their own destructive powers. People do it to other people, and humans do it to animals.

What does this actually mean? Well, in order to exert influence, will, control, very harsh measures are taken to achieve a desired outcome in the person who it is being inflicted upon.

The effect this has is to literally break someone's spirit. This means a piece or pieces of the soul break away because they cannot cope with the situation, and the person becomes diminished and damaged for life.

When a piece of soul is missing, the power of the person is much less. They do not function properly and are open to further attack and mental and physical illness. The piece or pieces of soul will stay lost for the whole of that person's life and, if not reconnected, will continue from lifetime to lifetime until such time as the energetic reconnection takes place.

So in what circumstances does this happen? Well, parents can do this to their children, husband to wives and vice versa, teachers to pupils, bosses to their employees. Some bosses will systematically break the spirit of their subordinates to gain their influence. This happens in large corporations to small firms. It happens in prisons, schools, care homes, colleges, in all societies. It will happen anywhere where people are given power. These people who inflict the bullying and tyranny and have issues around controlling others are themselves damaged souls.

Historically, the armed forces are one of the main culprits for breaking the spirits of the young men and women in their care. The reasons why are not up for debate in this content. I am trying to point out that it is an accepted method of control and what long-lasting damage it inflicts. It is up to the reader to decide if this is the type of behavior that we wish to continue in our society. As I have mentioned, this has gone on for generations, and it means there are many souls incarnating with aspects of themselves missing.

Can you mend a broken spirit or, to put it another way, be reconnected to your missing soul pieces? The answer is yes, people with soul fragmentation can be put back together again. The question which has to be asked is does this apply to me. You may feel that something is missing, that you are not whole. You may look to others for clues as to how to behave, you may just know that something is not right with yourself but cannot determine what.

My Personal Story

My father abandoned me. The one person who a girl worships is her father. He was supposed to be my protector. To teach me about love by the way he should have loved me. To talk to me about boys and men.

My broken relationship with my father, my broken spirit at an early age led me to becoming a people pleaser. Looking for the love of my father in everyone else. Seeking validation, love, and self-worth.

Not knowing that I was on a path of destruction.

People Pleasers are people who put needs of others before their own. I ended up doing things that I would never do now that I have learned to like and love myself.

I remember this one relationship I was in. I dressed the way my boyfriend wanted me to. Wearing short mini skirts, no jeans, and shorts where you could almost see my butt cheeks. Pleasing him and all the while, I felt uncomfortable because this wasn't me.

Signs of a People Pleaser

- You agree with everyone when you really don't.
- You take responsibility for how people feel.
- You apologize often when it's not even your fault.

- You feel stressed by the things you have to do.
- You have a hard time saying no.
- You feel sad and fear if someone is angry at you.
- You act like the people around you.
- You need compliments to feel good.
- You don't like conflict and avoid it at all cost.
- You hate and fear being hurt.

Common Signs of People Pleasing

Had I known the common signs of people pleasing, I probably would've been able to stop my exhausting behavior sooner. Here are some common signs of people pleasing, as well as more information about the people-pleaser personality.

- You have a hard time saying no because you feel guilty or too worried about the other person's feelings.
- You are quick to say yes and sometimes find it really hard to follow through with everything you committed to.
- White lies have been used to help you get out of obligations you over-committed to.
- Sorry is a common word in your vocabulary.
- You find it hard to accept help or compliments.
- Rescuing people – at work, in relationships – gives you a sense of purpose and validation, but often leaves you feeling burnt out and exhausted.

- You have a hard time communicating what you truly want or need to be fully happy.

My relationships with men and boys were terrible. I took whatever came to me. Disrespect, mental and verbal abuse. The constant put-downs of why don't you do this or that. You are not smart enough! You are nothing like my last girlfriend. Can you do this for me? Having sex even when I wasn't in the mood. Thinking and feeling if I give my boyfriend everything he wants that in turn I would get everything I needed, and that was love.

It didn't work! I couldn't live up not only to his expectations but others as well. The more you do for people to make them happy, the more they want from you. They wanted perfection.

I lived my life for everyone. I lost or really never knew who the real me was! I lived in fear of not being liked or accepted. So, I played it safe. I never took chances. I missed so many opportunities. Being a cheerleader, basketball player, model, actor, runner, etc.

People Pleasers - How to Deal with Other People's Problems

Become More Assertive

Every day, use the few quiet moments between waking and rising from your bed to re-educate your mind: to teach yourself to think differently.

Think about your value as a person - not in terms of what you do in the way of solving other people's problems - but in the gifts and skills you bring to life.

Value yourself - not for what you DO, but for the caring person you ARE.

Ask yourself: what are the choices for life that are open to me? Now ask, what is my lifestyle choice? In other words, what do you want in life? Perhaps you've always wanted to go back to college. To take up golf. To travel more. Make a plan. Put it into action.

If you recognize in yourself a gift for helping others, make up your mind to use it in a structured manner: perhaps by teaching a class on a craft, becoming a teacher's assistant in a school, helping in a charity shop.

In this way, new pathways of thinking will be laid down in your brain. You are, literally, learning to re-educate yourself.

Learn to give yourself thinking time when you're asked to help with other people's problems. Learn to say, 'I'll have to look at my diary' or 'I'll give you a ring when I've checked with Michael/Mildred.' Learn to say no - graciously, without making excuses, without feeling guilty.

Practice, practice, practice. Practicing is an active part of learning, which is crucial to success. If possible, enlist the help of your family.

Every time a situation arises in which other people have expectations of you, question the validity of their demands. Learn to evaluate what is reasonable.

If you find yourself slipping back into old habits and feel bad about yourself, or other people, learn to turn the negative thoughts into positive ones. Not, 'No one appreciates me!' but 'I did a good job planting out all those bulbs - and I loved every minute of it!'

And finally, we're told to love our neighbor (that's anyone who crosses our path - family, friends, and others) as ourselves. But if you don't love yourself, you can't truly love others. And if you don't love yourself, then neither will others love you.

Life as a Recovering People Pleaser

After a lot of self-development books, yoga, meditation, and personal reflection, I am a proud recovering people pleaser. Someone who is not afraid to say no, but more importantly, I am someone who is no longer afraid to say yes.

I have finally regained control of my power, and my anxiousness to please no longer defines me. Instead, I love harder, I say no more often, and I make sure that, in the end, I am taken care of because I am worth it.

And so are you.

People Pleasing Personality

Today, I am a self-care coach (I attended many Institutes on this) and co-author of this book. I am passionate about helping people – like you – who give too much to everyone around them, leaving nothing for yourself by the end of the day.

A person who is tired, stressed-out, and way too hard on himself/herself. You pour precious energy and resources into clothes, happy hours, people, and work in search of the life you crave. The life without fear of rejection and fear of failure, the life where poor self-esteem is a thing of the past.

161

When All You Know Is People Pleasing

See, the funny thing is most people pleasers are so used to people pleasing and catering to the needs of others they forget what they truly want. Over time, you might lose touch with your authentic values and find communicating your needs as a people pleaser as next to impossible.

People pleasing is truly a vicious cycle of seeking affirmation and positive feedback from those around us, which we receive by obliging to their wishes. After living that life for months, you might find yourself harboring resentment for those you've been so quick to help in the past. You might even convince yourself that they're the inconsiderate ones and can't understand how other people can be so rude.

As hard as it is to hear, in most cases, it's not the other person's fault for your unhappiness. It all comes back to common people pleasing behavior and lack of communication, low self-esteem, and fear of rejection on your end.

If this is resonating with you, it's important to remember that you are worthy of happiness, and saying no to things that don't bring you joy doesn't make you a bad person. Remember what your values are and reassess what you've been prioritizing as important. Self-care is a tool that can help you move away from your people-pleasing behavior and transition into living the life of a recovering people pleaser.

Take a moment to look back over your life to this point in time. How many times have you tried to please someone else? How many times has it been that you have succeeded in pleasing that person? Has it really been worth all the trouble you went through to try to please them? Most likely the answer you will have to that last question is most probably No. So, why bother trying to do it? Why not start concentrating on doing the things that please you? You are here on this earth to enjoy your life, not to be dictated to by somebody else. You deserve to be happy just as much as every other person in this world does, so now is the time to start making it happen. Stop worrying so much about what other people think and start focusing on the things that make you happy.

To Protect and Serve

Tiffany Quinn

My parents were married when they were eighteen years old, and they separated after having three children born to their union, and just to make a long story short, my mom had care of my brother and me. My maternal grandparents could've protected us, but that would've meant that my mom would've had to move back to Cleveland. Nevertheless, my mother wanted to remain independent. She chose to stay in Chicago, and finally in 1967, Mom moved to Michigan and worked as an auto assembly worker at General Motors Buick City. My dad could've protected us; he only lived a couple of hours away in Chicago. I had seen him infrequently as a young child.

We had little money, but we always had food and, thanks to our mother's cooking skills, decent clothing. I took pride in helping my mom with household chores on weekends, enthusiastically vacuuming the floors and doing laundry in the wringer washer in the basement. I was around 8 years old when you scared me and changed my childhood dreams. My brother asked me if it was true. I showed him the peep holes in the walls from the bedroom. He said, I will protect you. We just wondered how come he was trying to hurt me and why you weren't protecting me. It hurt me so badly that I started to talk to others about what occurred that night. I was in my bedroom. I was in my bed. My home, a place I should have felt safe and secure. You were a family friend, everybody loved and trusted you, and so you took advantage of it. Mom, where are you? I am scared. Mom, you finally left this man. Now, I feel protected. He died, now we are all safe.

I got pregnant at 17, and shortly after turning 18, I graduated from Beecher High School class of 1982 and then, I gave birth to my son and became a single mom. For three years. I worked hard to make ends meet, juggling living expenses with the cost of college. I dressed my son in secondhand clothes and bought toys from yard sales. When I had work late at night, I would take him to my mom's house and then leave him for the entire weekend. I moved us into a small one-bedroom apartment on Detroit Street. With my preoccupation with lack of money and being on welfare, I barely noticed the apartment manager eyeballing me as he explained how to make ends meet.

During my first night in the apartment, I realized I didn't want to live alone, so I was going let my boyfriend, my son's father, move in with me. I wanted to feel safe and protected. I wanted my son to have his father in the home. Baby Daddy's talking about getting together and meeting up at the apartment. Later that evening, I went to the apartment and waited—with no furniture, no phone and, now, a no-show. I walked down to the pay phone to see if he was still coming through. I waited up so late that I eventually fell asleep. I was awaken to someone getting on top of me and covering my mouth and putting a knife to my neck, saying, "Don't move. I know who you are, and I have your identification. I will kill you!" I was violated and raped.

It's taken me a long time to write this, 10 years in fact. But the time is right to share my story in an attempt to move on. Ten years ago today—it's still as clear now as it was then. The pain, the violation, the same questions-why me? How did this happen? Why didn't I try harder to get away? To make him stop? Why did I stay? I was 17. Immediately after the rape, I called my mother, and with her support, I went to the hospital to report the crime and undergo a medical exam. I found it helpful to study trauma, and so I sought rehabilitation through education and therapy. For the sake of the story, I am leaving out a lot of sadness and significant issues within the story.

I went on to marry and have two children by this same boyfriend. The marriage didn't work out, and we divorced after 10 years.

In therapy, I would talk about my trauma as if I were a completely different person. It was the only way that I could think about it without falling apart.

After being assaulted in college, I was diagnosed with post-traumatic stress disorder. After years in therapy, trying different medications, learning to reinforce boundaries with friends and family (and even professors), I am finally making lasting progress.

Now, as a Ph.D. student of theology, I am not standing on top of the Genesee Towers garage, contemplating jumping off of the edge. I have not had a nightmare since the Lord healed me, though I still sometimes have issues sleeping through the night. These days, I am fairly consistent with my work. I am able to talk about my trauma research without anxiety. My self-worth was intertwined with my performance in the classroom. School was where I felt confident and safe. I excelled. Due to my disability, I have experienced public shaming, condescending lectures, and slights against my character. It is all very defeating. I find myself begging faculty members to have faith in me and apologizing for things that are outside of my control. And just to be clear: my disorder makes me stronger and more capable than most people. Even when I do spiral into a shame hole and fall into depression, I am still strong.

Even on my worst day, I know deep down that I am an extraordinary servant. It takes a commitment to God, patience, and compassion to heal from trauma. Most important, recovery requires support from professionals, family, friends, and even institutions.

I tell my own story, without shame, as I reach out to other women around the world, encouraging them to tell theirs.

You = Power…
Rise Up!

Chanel Spencer

When I was a child, I would hear things like, "Chanel, when you grow up, you can accomplish anything you set your mind to. You can be anyone you want to be." Statements like this became whispers of encouragement that echoed in my mind throughout my childhood. I believed them. I received them as my truth.

When we tell a child if they stretch high enough they can reach the stars, we rarely include how difficult the journey might be to get there. Those who encouraged me wished to see me flourish, to reach my full potential, to realize my power, and use it to make the world a better place. However, they didn't mention the adversity we face in this life and did not equip me with the tools I needed to overcome the obstacles I faced. When they looked at me as a small child, innocent and undefiled from this world, they identified a piece of themselves. The person buried deep within them, muted and hidden under layers of hurt, pain, and disappointments. Stripped of their power and left to wait it out in the rusty cage where hopes and dreams go to perish. When that person, entombed within, saw the spark of existence in my eyes, they wanted to fan my flame, hoping once I rose in all my power, maybe, just maybe it would be enough to reignite their fire and free them from their own prison.

When I entered my young adult years, I failed to notice the subdued sound of promise had been slowly transformed into a booming echo from the cage that engulfed me. The message of hope and optimism somehow turned into unreachable expectations, creating a tendency in me to push through, regardless of the circumstances I experienced. I lost connection with my dreams. I no longer believed the promise of good things for my life. I learned how to push through, at any cost, but I had shut down emotionally, numbing myself.

One circumstance didn't cause the sweet whisper of hope to transform into the bars I found surrounding me. Rather, a combination of events took place, slowly stripping me of my dreams. Being molested at a young age robbed me of my innocence. Kids bullied me for being too thin and developing much later than my peers. This caused me to question my beauty and worth. I didn't feel like I fit anywhere. People said I wasn't attractive enough. I wasn't smart enough. I wasn't good enough. I believed them. Suddenly, I knew I wasn't enough.

I found myself in an abusive relationship that beat me down physically and emotionally, robbing me of any shred of dignity and aspiration I had left. Eventually, I became a single mother, struggling in every sense of the word. I didn't have time to dream; I had to fight to stay alive, to survive.

The narrative of my life was so far removed from the dream the delicate whisper had inspired. I was living an unrecognizable existence that felt controlled by someone else. People I thought loved me, little by little, drained every ounce of power I had left. I was a long way from recognizing my worthiness, incapable of seeing I deserved unconditional love. I lost myself. I fell into a heavy depression. I was stressed beyond belief and physically exhausted from the continual push to move forward despite everything I had been through. I was mentally and emotionally broken, ready to give up. When I thought it couldn't get any worse, it did. I found myself at my lowest point, shattered from abuse and unsure if I had a life worth saving.

And then, out of nowhere, there it was. The tender whisper nudged me ever so slightly. For just one moment, I remembered I once had a dream for my life. I could have ignored the nudge, but I didn't. I made a conscious decision to rise, to get up, to restore my power. Like a phoenix rises from the ashes, I burst out of captivity, determined to realign with my dream and call the power I allowed to be drained back to myself.

I wish I could say that overnight I became a different person, but the road of restoration was long. The healing work I required was intense. Every day, I had to wake up actively making the choice to be the best version of myself. I had to make the active choice to live. I learned how to stop pushing through and how to feel my feelings. I learned how to work through and release pain and negative emotions. I stopped numbing myself and opened myself up to love, self-love. I saw my worth, and I quit giving my power away. I got support. I knew I needed tools to aid in my healing. Even though I was scared to death,

I took the brave step to find someone to guide me through the healing process.

I have four mantras that carry me through each day: I am powerful, I am strong, I am beautiful, and I am successful. They are the whispers I listen to as I rise in the morning, and they are on repeat throughout my day. In the depths of my soul, I know my mantras are true; they have become a part of my DNA. There have been so many moments I almost threw in the towel, but the sweet whisper of my mantras would remind me who I was and enable me to acknowledge the sometimes very dim light at the end of the tunnel so I could rise and fight again. If I am knocked down 200 times, I have resolved that I will rise 201!

I share my story so you will understand your circumstances, past or present, do not define you. Your choices cannot imprison you. People cannot take your power. You are responsible for how you react to the world around you. If you don't like the narrative of your life, change it. You are the author of your story and can write yourself into a fresh chapter at any moment. Every morning, I make the choice to rise up. Even if I cried myself to sleep the night before, even if I feel depressed, even when I don't want to move at all, I rise up. When I feel like giving up, burnt out, and like the world is coming to the end, I still choose to rise up! We all have choices in this life, and we need to understand that our circumstances do not determine our destiny. Life will throw storms, hurricanes, and maybe even tsunamis your way, but every day, you get to make the choice to rise up.

I want women and girls to realize that together we can break generational cycles of abuse and reclaim our power. Each of us, regardless of our race and socioeconomic status, can open our ears to hear the whispers of the hope that once was. We can allow the gentle whispers to arouse the flame, causing a combustion within us so we can rise up into the powerful women we are created to be. Remember, YOU=POWER! You are powerful; You are strong; You are beautiful; You are successful. RISE UP!

Keepin' the Faith

Broken to Be Healed

Kesia Carter

When I was released out of my mother's womb, I entered a sinful, promiscuous world that was and is constantly seeking love from all the wrong places. During the time my father and mother met, my mom was just getting out of a marriage with a bigamist who had five wives. Mom and Dad met in St. Louis, MO. My father is an Arkansas native, and my mother was born and raised in Georgia; they both moved to Boston, MA. And that is where the root of **Abandonment** took place. My father and mother split when I was 3. I can still remember it to this day, looking out of a window, crying for my daddy. What do you do as a child? a teenager? a young adult? or just an adult with childhood attachment issues that have never been addressed? Self-consciously, you begin to invite what is diabolical and devious to intrude a vessel that has a broken heart part. This heart part is so broken that it allows our human nature to attempt to replace the pain, discomfort, and emptiness, with a *lie*.

With that being addressed, as soon as that fine dark and handsome man approaches you and tells you that he wants to love you, and that you are everything he desires, you will then lose sight of who God has called you to be. That is what happened to me at the age of fifteen; that 3-year-old reappeared and was in search of her daddy's love. What sounds good is not what is always good for you. People may present themselves with a presence of light; however, they can also operate in everything that is dark. This is how the door of *domestic violence* opened for me. As a three-time *domestic violence survivor*, I had to learn how to love myself without abuse. You name it, I had experiences with physical, emotional, sexual, verbal, and financial abuse that came in from every way, with boyfriends and husbands.

My last *domestic violence* experience took place three years ago; this experience allowed me to transition into the creative, innovative, loving, and caring women I am today. The only way I was able to get my healing was to go straight to God for deliverance. I needed deliverance in so many areas. Even as a Christian woman, I was still doing things in my own right, which was obviously wrong. I learned that having a desire to want and love an individual greater than God is *idolatry*. Putting something or someone before our Abba (Father) is detrimental to our well-being. I also learned that *disobedience* can kill you. Well, I did just that, and it bought me so much pain. In every aspect of my life, I was broken. That is when I went to God for complete healing, and the answer he gave me was this: "Kesia, I am going to teach you how to love yourself the way I love you, and in return, you will teach others to love themselves the way I (God) love them."

I was struck with joy and confusion all at the same time. I was wondering how that could ever happen. Shortly after, the Lord started giving me sermons and scriptures and said to go on radio with this message of love. I then asked God, "What do I name this part of my mission?" He answered, "Love Thy Self Radio Ministries." Today, this platform is for the public to talk about the God given Kingdom Assignment, Purpose, and Plan that God has for us as individuals as *he* is teaching us how to love ourselves. During this journey, God gave me a Treatment Plan that can be implemented into anyone's life who is ready for *his* change to take place. I utilized this treatment plan for a whole year and saw the great manifestation of God showing up in every area of my life. Of course, I had to rebuke and denounce many things that I had opened up, but nevertheless…baby, sugar pie, honey bunch, once I closed those doors and applied the *TRUTH* (God's word along with the treatment plan), I became a *New Creature* in *Christ Jesus*. I am living a free delivered life today; however, I am still a work in progress!

Have a Little Faith

Rita Casman

Hope is the last resource. Faith needs hope and is renewed every day just as neurons in our brains.

They say that the last thing that's lost is hope; it's what keeps us living and what creates faith. I've been thinking a lot about it lately, how faith may seem like a fantasy. However, faith is something that we create in reality with the help of our brain, an instrument that God created not only to be part of our bodies, but also to keep us going. That is why mental health is so important, and the stigma must be broken.

How can the uncertain seem so certain with faith? Our mind is a tool that we must learn about and take charge of it. Our thoughts do become our reality because we don't even have to believe something; as long as we repeat it, our mind thinks it must be true; therefore, it eventually becomes a reality.

I had no idea what faith really was until I started studying how we create it. Faith is a belief that we bring in our lives. We are not perfect, so sometimes faith can be as small as a mustard seed, but hey! That is all we need to start with. I love the fact that our mind can be renewed every single day; it's in books, healthcare studies, and the Bible.

Now, let's get into the juicy part. I sound pretty positive, right? You are reading this from a woman that was cured from ovarian cancer and is currently battling endometriosis stage 4, had advanced issues with her spine, and is recuperating from dissociative and borderline personality disorder among other things like being bullied at school, having a suicide attempt at school when she was 12, having an abortion at 23, and cancelling a wedding at 25. Boo. Tragedy. Sounds scary, right? All of this was done by work and faith that allowed God's power to unleash in my life; therefore, his will is perfect.

The connection that God created between our body, mind and soul is magnificent. Knowledge is power, and that is what has set me free. Life always brings us tests that keep us moving up on higher levels, no matter how well we are doing. Nothing lasts forever. Note that it only gets better because once we have passed certain situations, we don't get to get them again. Many times, it depends on what we need to accomplish and what we are capable of handling. We are all very different, so we can't compare ourselves.

My worst enemy was my mind. I changed my mind by making it my best friend. When you're a kid or a naïve teenager/adult, like I used to be, it's very probable that you won't know about your mind's secrets. It's a mystery. You have to be ready to let it in, so it doesn't matter if you're young or old. It took me 34 years of my life, a lot of trials and studies.

When I was 4 years old, I was sexually abused a few times by the father of a dear friend of my family.

I kept it for seven years; only my mother knew. That is one of the things that mostly messed up my mind because it made me do things that I didn't want to. It was also the reason for all of my health issues. It took me years to forgive, and it changed completely the way that other events – such as my father's murder – were taken in my life experience.

I started therapy when I was 17, but since I was living in my hometown of Guatemala City, Guatemala in Central America, it made it difficult because my insurance wouldn't cover it. My mom offered help back when I was 11, and at that time, the dissociative disorder was being very convenient for me as all of the pain was stored in a very spider-web place very hidden in my brain. So, I grew up broken but putting myself together with God's help. The problem was that after a while, I was self-medicating with overspending, alcohol, partying, unprotected sex, and other related addictions.

A friend of mine once told me I looked happy, but that beneath my happy face, there was something much deeper. She was right. The good thing is that God never ever gives us more time on a test than we cannot overcome or take more of.

The beginning of my new beginning started seven years ago when I became an entrepreneur.

I started working when I was 18, and almost ten years later, I started to remind myself of what I really wanted to do with my life. I always knew that I was an entertainer. Unfortunately, our criteria are impacted by our surroundings, making me confused on really going for it. I would say to myself "Maybe in two years, maybe next year." Sometimes, I would think maybe never, until the time came for my life purpose to become a reality.

Even though I was unsure of what decision to take, I was pretty sure it had to be something creative and artistic, so I went for communication and design for my bachelor's degree. I have always been a little nerd, so I took a few MBA courses and later got my master's in international relations, diplomacy and public image. This was the turning point for me. I started getting very tired of being a marketing consultant; I only saw it as a temporary job and not as my passion.

One of my last clients was a former Hollywood special effects director and artist. One day working late at the office, I had a little lightbulb turn on inside me, and I Googled Acting Classes in Los Angeles. Turns out that now you can even get a master's degree on it. I didn't even think about the money when I made a pact with God. It was the first time that I relied all of my trust in him. I asked him to make his will mine and that if this was for me, to make it happen – and it did.

A bonus came with my wish as well. A man – who's now my husband. He has made me American in every single way that I could have possibly imagined. It has been tough, but we stick together every single step of the way. America has saved me in so many ways, which I must include my mental and physical health. Becoming an immigrant is something out of this world. However, I was getting longer, and more frequent, depressive episodes, and I was even contemplating suicide. It started to get dangerous at the point where hope and faith were a must in my life and the tools to get me out of that rabbit hole.

I started asking God what to do because I felt that I was stuck, so he gave me a revelation. I needed to overcome fear, be creative, and study to become free of the captivity that I found myself in. I became like Joseph the dreamer, doing something that would also buy my time out while I am released to do what God sent me to do – tell others' stories through mine. So, I did what he told me to do instead of just waiting. I even started reading books and taking related courses. Now that I know myself, I changed to the right version of me – the brave one.

I don't know what you have gone through or what you are going through. What I do know is that I must recommend you not only to try out God, but also to look for whatever helps you cope. As you can read, I used a series of tools that were not only self-help, they also required me to accept help. God created people to help us; we are never alone. God's angel is always with you and will always be with you. Just have a little faith and remember that hope keeps you going.

"It's not easy, but it's not impossible either." -Rita in the film, *Shadow Wall*

Hoe to Wholesome

Angel Colbert

Cleavage out, tight clothes wearing, drunker than a skunk, high as a kite, bad decision making, using your body to get what you want hoe. I have always done what I wanted to, especially if I didn't think it affected anyone else. I told the truth, for the most part, unless we are counting white lies, and I was good on my word. I believed in doing to others as they do to you. I believed in a higher power but felt like all you had to do was practice love and kindness, and the Universe would provide all my wants and needs. Church really wasn't my thing because of all the hypocrites, and it just didn't make much sense because of what the people who were sitting in the pulpit were doing in the world.

Enough about them, this is about me. I also had premarital sex, had a child out of wedlock, committed adultery, and was very much a pleaser of my flesh. The adultery almost cost me my marriage. We are always one decision away from our lives turning out very different one way or the other. Committing adultery involves more than just yourself, and the effects can hurt your entire family and others' family as well, feelings get involved, and you have no idea where others' minds go. I became manipulative to get what I wanted and made it like it was my husband's fault as to why I was having a bad day or doing the things I did. Although he had his ways, I made my own decisions. We all fall short, and when we know better, we should do better. "All have sinned and are not good enough to share God's divine greatness. They are made right with God by his grace. This is a free gift. They are made right with God by being made free from sin through Jesus Christ" (Romans 3:23-24, ERV). For me to change, I had to worry about myself; only person you can change is you.

The way God decided to show me told me he was real, that it was him and not the universe or just any old higher power. This was an experience that I have been having trouble putting into words. It was like nothing I have ever experienced in my life. God clearly had other plans for my life: "For I know the plans I have for you, declares the LORD, plans to prosper you and not to harm you, plans to give you hope and a future" (Jeremiah 29:11). He decided to show me how controlling I was, how impatient I was, and how manipulative I was, showing me all of this in the middle of an act of adultery. I was cumming, and God was calling. *Right now, God?* I thought. *Can I call you back in about an hour?* I have never squirted, and that had always been a goal of mine, and when I tell you this was the moment, or so I thought. I fully let go of the control and let my male partner take control, I trusted him with every being in my soul to get the job done. Everything I had read about squirting talked about relaxing, clearing your mind, and not to worry about anything. I did just that, I was in the most euphoric state I had ever been in. To the point that I even allowed my no zone to be licked. Which are my ears. My ears are very sensitive, and I never let my ears be a part of four play. That was the key to Pandora's box. It was like I was traveling in space to another time. I started to see my life in a movie reel past, present, and future. My past, losing my virginity, the day before my 13th birthday, my parents getting a divorce, and the death of my brother. My present adulterous lifestyle, my personality, and my manipulative ways. My future if I continued on the dark path I was on, and if I followed God's path. Both paths had an outcome of prosperity. Although if I continued down the path I was on, my family would have been disappointed in my decisions, and most of all, a disgrace to God. The more I was seeing, the more intense things were getting. I am a nurse and have a patient who has regular seizures; I imagined myself looking like she did when in the middle of a seizure. I did not have control of my body; I could no longer even feel what my male partner was doing. I was in the matrix. I was not in my body is the only way I can explain it. Finally, as I was trying to find my words to say stop, I yelled PEPSI, PEPSI, PEPSI. This was the safe word. If you don't have a safe word, you better get you one. This twenty-first century awakening sex ain't no joke. My heart beat out of my chest. I was out of breath and totally disoriented. All I knew was I needed to apologize for my manipulation.

I received my first download from God, and I thought I was certified crazy. I was talking different, and I had all these different thoughts about my family

185

and their issues. As the days went on, things that had been downloaded into me I learned were true, and things that had happened I knew were going to happen. The fear of the Lord was placed in my heart when my mother verified some things that happened to her and that she did surrounded in rape and molestation. "Knowledge begins with fear and respect for the LORD, but stubborn fools hate wisdom and refuse to learn (Proverbs 1:7, ERV). Things I had no idea about that happened to my mother and that she did, things that you don't really want to know about your mother. This information connected the dots about my own promiscuity, personality, and issues. These were seeds planted at birth via my generational issues. Old saying is "The apple doesn't fall far from the tree."

"Everything that is hidden will become clear. Every secret thing will be made known, and everyone will see it" (Luke 8:17).

My mother comes from a generation that sweeps things under the rug, and that is what has gotten us broken as a society. We need to talk about our issues so that we help the next generation instead of burying them. Our honesty will help other people become free of their insecurities and issues, and help our children not to go through the things we may have gone through.

Get up and win by sharing your story, talk about it, and help someone else. Break the barriers and choose to grow and be free from past trauma. Do not let the trauma be an EXCUSE to do things you know are wrong. You are only losing at your own life. The trials that may have happened to you, you weren't the first or the last, but this is your personal testimony. I can say I got it from my mother, or it was because of some life experiences that I did what I did and made the choices I made, but where will that get me? How will that help me grow? It won't. Yes, all those things are valid, but they are just that, excuses. You have a life to live in this world, you have a purpose to live out, and you will get nowhere with providing excuses. Use the trials and tribulations to move yourself ahead, use that as your passion. Market yourself with the knowledge you have gained in the experiences. This is how we get up and win! Change your mindset. These things didn't happen to you, they happened *for* you. Perception is everything; you choose how you will perceive a situation. All the things you have ever dreamed of doing and all the goals you haven't completed, now is the time to do them and WIN. You will never win if you don't even get in the game.

Face Your Fears and Allow Faith to Keep You

Dr. Cortesha Cowan

Before she knew herself, God knew her; the "her" I am referring to is me...Dr. Cortesha Cowan. I learned very early in life that faith has kept me, and my faith continues to sustain me [this was imperative]. I also had to understand the nine fruits of the spirit as they are detailed in the Word of God. If you don't know the nine fruits of the spirit, I encourage you to read Galatians 5:20 -23... allow it to bless and educate you! Although all the nine fruits of the spirit are significant, faithfulness constantly surfaces as a necessity of having a successful walk with God! I keep a notepad with me at all times because God *literally* downloads profound narratives about "keeping the faith." The insight He provides continually blows my mind!

Consider the word *pistols* (Greek) meaning to be trusted, reliable, to be depended on continually, and of a firm and faithful persuasion. This tells me that God trusts us to have faith and trust in Him. Allow the following anecdote to reveal the power of faithfulness. Growing up, there were times in my life that I *had* to trust God [I felt I had no other choice], especially when I became a teenage mother. I had to know that God had me and the innocent child He entrusted me with [even in my iniquity]; premarital sex was my sin–NOT my child. Children are always a blessing from God [Psalm 127:3-5 *Children* are a heritage from the LORD, offspring are a reward from Him]. However, I was not rich, but God made a way out of no way so many times. I have kept *this* kind of faith in my life. I knew the Holy Spirit was *always* with me, even when my faith was the size of a microscopic mustard seed.

You… the one reading this, GOD has you as well! However, He wants you to keep the faith. Faith takes us further than our resources, logic, money, and/or relationships. Faith and Faithfulness are eternally linked… This is how: Have you ever sung the song "Great Is Thy Faithfulness, Great Is Thy Faithfulness" by Thomas Chisholm? Faithfulness is the working out of the inner belief [faith] that we possess. Conversely, faith is the foundation to everything that we believe and act upon. Faith is the undeniable power that is realized because we cannot see it [initially]. When we have real faith in God, we genuinely respond in the most faithful way we know how. As the word says, "Faith without works is dead." If you ask someone what faith is, you will receive a variety of responses. Most people will say faith means to trust or believe in someone or something. However, this is only part of it. To fully understand faith, it is imperative to study. Take a closer look at the word faith in the book of Hebrews; read chapter 11, verses 1-40. I believe this narration provides the best breakdown of faith from a biblical context. When I educate others about faith, I ask them to write down the definition of faith in their own words. I want you to do the same; as you read this chapter, take some time to thoroughly define faith from a personal perspective.

I know how to apply faith in my everyday living. Do you know what faith "looks like" in your day to day activities? How do you apply and/or exercise faith in your life? I wrote this chapter on faith because I believe we need to understand how much further we would be if only we held onto our faith through the storms, the pitfalls, and the uncertainties. When things "go south" in my life, I PRAY and tell God that I *still* have faith. I tell Him that I believe in His love and guidance for my life. I express the urgency of my need of Him, by letting Him know that I know my faith in Him MAKES all things become possible! Faith helps us UNDERSTAND and continually RECOGNIZE who God is! Every time doubt rears its ugly head, I call on the Lord, and HE prays for me so that my faith in Him does not fail [Luke 22:32].

I talk to God all the time. It's much harder to see substantiated foundation without faith; this is a vital part of our lives. Please understand that it is extremely important that we keep our faith *faithfully*, and without it, we will collapse [spiritually]. Do you use faith when you're driving your car? Yes, you do! You have the faith no one will hit you. When you're at work, you have faith that your employer will pay you the following week or the week after. Thus, I have learned to use that same faith in every aspect of my life [from business to personal]. I have faith that the vision and plan that God has given me will come to pass in this life.

By faithfully walking out each day and every task set before me, I see the mighty hand of God working on my behalf. God is faithful; He does not change His provision is based on the magnitude of our faith [or lack thereof]; because God is faithful to His word, He cannot lie. Numbers 23:19 (KJV): [19] "God is not a man, that he should lie; neither the son of man, that he should repent: hath he said, and shall he not do it? or hath he spoken, and shall he not make it good?"

God gives us an incomparable and unconditional love that is eternally faithful, so as you progress through this chapter, please understand how necessary it is to *keep your faith*! If you're experiencing hardships in your life, communicate with God, spend time in His presence; there you will be strengthened and granted an indescribable peace. I continually encourage myself in the Word of God. In Psalms 46:1, it reads: "God is our refuge and strength, an ever-present help in trouble." Regardless of my circumstances, I know God will NOT fail me. I am here to tell you God is *with* you and *for* you. Our God is WITH us ALWAYS.

This doesn't mean our troubles will disappear and be easy to handle, but it does mean that God will walk with us through our trials. God promises to stick with us and provide encouragement, love, hope, and a reminder of our potential *through* and beyond our current situation.

To trust God, we must first understand the nature of God and how He often works in our lives. God is sovereign. His love and wisdom exceed our ability to understand Him and His ways; [I Corinthians 1:25] "For what seems to be God's foolishness is wiser than human wisdom, and what seems to be God's weakness is stronger than human strength.

Consider Romans 8:35-39, God commands us to be strong and courageous. He loves us! God has promised us that He will never leave us nor for sake us, so keep the faith and know that your journey will not end prematurely–it does have an expected end! Apply faith to your life, for because of God 's love, you can start exercising your faith right now! He is *already* with you; God is waiting to guide you, protect you, and bless you. I pray that you have been encouraged and edified. I pray that you receive everything God has for you! I cannot think of anything more assuring than the Word of God–His word is indestructible and everlasting. Consequently, His plans for our lives must materialize–or God would be a liar… we know that is impossible because the Word declares, "God is the way, the truth, and the life" [John 14:16].

As you carry out on this next journey, remain connected to God… the Word is your roadmap to success. Without it, the road you're traveling will be much harder. I know God led you to this book. Be blessed by each chapter and take heed. Reserve time to meditate and read over this chapter, allow it to compel change in your life. This is just a small nugget of all that God has for you. The abundance of blessings and provision that your faith can and will access will leave you constantly in awe of God's goodness. May God bless you on your walk of faithfulness as you go forth.

P.S. Faith will bring you through; trust the process you are in, for you are in one of the most pivotal places in your life. God knows the path, so let Him guide you. Surround yourself with believers who will build you up and encourage you to press despite the trials. Sometimes, all we need is a faithful friend to stand by us; that friend in this season needs to be God. Trust God and keep the faith when the future seems unclear. Understand that God is with you. Strive diligently into *your* new season and let your faith in God minister to you—because He is eternally faithful!

Fight to Keep Fighting!

Angel Robinson-Hubbard

What are you hoping for? Does there seem to be more stumbling blocks and obstacles standing in front of you than open doors? Welcome to this thing we call life, where you are going to have to fight the good fight of faith to get to where you want to be. I feel like once we all understand that, our journey will become a lot easier.

I came to that realization just recently as I found myself facing yet another obstacle. "All my life I had to fight," I exclaimed as I burst into laughter sharing my struggle with one of my brothers to help ease the pain. I was having a conversation with him similar to the one I often have with God. "Why do I have to fight for every stinking thing!? Haven't I fought enough already? I mean do you ever defeat the fighting level of the game?" In my mind, there should be a point where you just level off like okay, you spent 15 years plus of fighting...now the rest of your life is going to be full of bliss.

As we know, life doesn't quite work that way. It's full of obstacles, twist, and turns. However, when I really took a look at it, I realized that most opportunities and blessings I have experienced came right after some of the hardest obstacles that I faced and overcame.

Recently, my dad died. April 21, 2018, to be exact. The very same day that I had my latest public speaking event in Flint, MI. I had spent months preparing, promoting, networking, and planning for this event. "Bridging the Generational Gap" was the theme. I prepared for that day in every way I could. Yet I had not the slightest clue that minutes after I sighed the relief of having a successful event that I would be ushered into a cold quiet hospital room, looking at my dad's lifeless body on the bed like table. The moment seemed surreal.

The man who raised me, my fighter, my hero, my teacher, my protector...was gone. Yes, he gave me many speeches on how he would not always be here and that I must go on. He raised me as a single father and taught me how to survive, be strong, and independent. In his last serious conversation with me, he told me, "Keep going to church and take the kids even when they don't feel like going." All of his words of advice have hit me like a ton of bricks.

One of the hottest topics we had discussed in the months prior to him passing was me and my children relocating to Virginia. I could tell he wasn't too fond of the idea, but he still gave me his support.

June 18, 2018, a day after Father's Day, my three youngest children, myself and all that would fit in our gray 2008 Chevy Malibu left the city of Flint, the only home we knew, behind. It was a 14-hour drive with only one person old enough to drive, me. We did pretty good. Four stops to go to the restrooms and get gas and snacks.

The first month and a half, I felt such a sense of relief. I had a lot of time to think and process what I had just experienced. I had witnessed my dad dying, my first born graduate, and left everyone that I had ever known. It was a lot to process. I experienced the quiet and space I needed to breathe and heal. I was starting to feel whole again. I was finally able to rest. Not just the rest you acquire by sleeping; I was getting rest for my soul.

Things were going along pretty well. Then the end of July beginning of August came, and out of nowhere, another obstacle came. I had found myself and my three children without a place to stay. I was embarrassed, hurt, angry, and afraid. What in the world was I going to do? Surely, I did not want to tell anybody what I was going through. In my mind, that meant more shame, more rejection, more ridicule.

I remember sitting in a hotel room with my three children. After looking at the wall and window for hours straight, trying to muster up the wittiness and savviness I normally do when I'm in a bind only to realize I didn't have the resources I needed, I had not yet acquired a network, I didn't know where things were at. I didn't even have my "Ace in the hole" anymore, my dad. At that moment, I experienced a terror like no other come over me, and I said out loud in a tone that frightened me when it echoed back to me, "What am I going to do?"

So I did what my spiritual father said years ago, "When you don't know what to do, do what you DO know to do." I fell on my face, prostrate on the floor of the hotel room and worshipped and prayed. I uttered in my heavenly language, cried, and prayed over my kids. I felt such a sense of peace in the room afterwards. And although I still did not have an answer, I got up off the floor with so much comfort and authority.

Out of all the phone calls I made, I got one back that I never expected. My aunt, NB, had offered to help in a MAJOR way. I knew at the moment God was using her as an instrument to answer my prayer. Three weeks later, we were in our own home! All we had was three air mattresses and clothes.

During this whole process, we had also met some people from a church we had recently visited and a gentleman whom we had met while he was doing some community service at our temporary place of residence. Within the two weeks, they had all come together and blessed us tremendously. Our house became fully furnished! EVERYTHING we needed was brought to us from the beds, sheets, covers, towels, dishes, microwave, dining room table, lamps, living room furniture, you name it! On top of that, I had been having some trouble with my car, and they even fixed that. FREE OF CHARGE.

You can't tell me what God won't do for you if you just believe. When you are having a hard time in your life, don't fight people, don't beat yourself up. Fight the good fight of Faith. You will not always see your way out, but if you would just believe, God will continuously show you his Victory. "What, then shall we say in response to these things? If God is for us, who can be against us?" (Romans 8:31).

Faith and Hard Work

Ashley Little

Strong faith is key to being successful in all areas of our lives. I am a strong believer in faith and how it will change any situation. Girl, in order to "WIN" in life, you have to believe and put your faith in God. The more you elevate, the harder the attack, which is why the foundation has to be strong. We have to work in order for our faith to work, Faith without works is dead. We can't pray for stuff to happen without doing our part.

Girl, the road to success is an amazing journey, but you will have tests along the way. New levels bring new devils, and we have to be prepared to fight on our knees at all times. I have always been determined to step out on faith and take risks in order to accomplish my dreams. Whatever it takes as long as it is ethical has always been my mentality. However, I had to learn how to embrace the process, pain, and journey. One of the hardest things I had to overcome was being okay with being uncomfortable. I have had many seasons in my life where I didn't want to embrace it, but it was necessary. I remember times when I would try to take matters into my own hands, instead of submitting and surrendering to God fully.

198

Girl, I learned some hard lessons, and every time I thought I was in control, God would humble me. Learn from my mistakes, sis, and totally submit and surrender to God in everything you do. The worst lesson you want to experience is God humbling you because he knows how to get our attention.

In June 2018, I wrote my first book and became a published author, which gave my platform more exposure. This was the first time I was vulnerable with the world and shared some trials I had to overcome with the world. I always knew I had a story to tell the world, but I didn't act on it until last year. I'm so thankful I stepped out on faith and trusted the process to share my story in the world. You never know whose life you are going to change or save with your story. Throughout last year, as I continued to grow in every area of my life, I was tested. Some tests I passed, and some tests I had to repeat until I surrendered. When God is about to elevate you, tests will come, and it is up to us to recognize those tests. Satan tried to do everything he could to stop me from sharing my story with the world, but I refused to quit. God birthed one book that turned into four books by the end of 2018. Sis, anytime you are getting close to your destiny, attacks will come, so you have to stay strong and have faith. The main ingredient is your foundation; it has to be strong in order to get to the next level. Throughout my journey of entrepreneurship and authorpreneurship, I have learned a lot about people and being in alignment.

I work in corporate America by day and as a serial entrepreneur by night. I'm thankful for painful seasons I have experienced in corporate America because they pushed me out to entrepreneurship.

Going through many different seasons of discrimination as a black woman in corporate America prepared me for the storms of entrepreneurship. Working a 9to5 and building your dreams is not for the weak. It takes strong faith and a personal relationship with God. I have learned so many lessons on this road to entrepreneurship.

Some key things I have learned along the way is:

(1) To always put God first and completely submit and surrender to him. When we try to do things on our own, they will be temporary and will not last. When we do things God's way, it will have impact and purpose.

(2) Everyone is not going support you, and you have to be okay with that. We have to remember man does not control our destiny; God controls our destiny. We have to trust God and the process. When people revealed themselves to me, it was hurtful, but it was necessary. I had to focus on the big picture and trust that God would put the right people in my path.

(3) Elevation requires separation. Throughout the journey to success, you are going to have to walk alone to get to the top. Embrace the process and understand eagles fly alone. When people walk away, let them go and understand when their time is up, it's not a bad thing. As, I continue to elevate, God has revealed a lot of people who I thought had my back. It takes strong faith, work, and foundation to keep pushing and building your dreams. You have to ignore the distractions and pass the tests.

(4) Rejection is part of the process; don't be afraid of rejection, girl, it comes with the territory. I don't know one successful person who has not failed. Failure is a lesson; you learn from it and do better

next time. If you haven't failed, you haven't been successful. Always "Shoot your Shot," and if you get a no, keep going. You only live once.

(5) Moving in silence is essential to your success. Girl, you have to learn how to be quiet and execute. Everyone is not going to be happy for you, and that's okay. People don't have to like you, but they will respect you. It kills people when they don't know your moves and business. Keep them wondering, and let success make the noise.

(6) Stay humble because if you don't, life or God will humble you. I'm speaking from experience. When we try to do things our way, I am a living breathing testimony that it will not work. When I was going through my seasons of discrimination in corporate America, I tried to fight the process and do things my way. I was so uncomfortable in those seasons. I experienced many different emotions, such as anger, depression, rejection, wanting to quit, but I had to humble myself and totally surrender to God. I look back at those seasons, and I am so thankful I didn't quit. If I would have quit in the middle of the process, I wouldn't be able to share my story with you. Those seasons pushed me into my destiny, and I am so thankful. Now, when I am faced with trials, I embrace the pain because I know it is a part of the process.

Lastly, "Girl, Get Up And Win." You only live once. Your only competition is yourself. Embrace being uncomfortable, and don't be afraid to walk alone. Invest in mentors and coaches who are where you want to be in life. Do your research on people, and make sure you are aligning yourself with the right people. Always remember your "Network is your Networth." Stay focused, shoot your shot, fight on your knees, and remember, hard work requires strong faith and many sacrifices. Girl, let's WIN together!

Rebounding After a Fall

Twana Matthews

Have you ever had a life experience that wounded you so bad that all you could say was, "What happened?" or "How did I fall into this mess?" I have, and I am here to tell you that it don't feel good.

You see, my life has been difficult at times. During those times, I found myself in the middle of chaos, conflict, and complete disorder. Confusion was all around me, which caused my body and mind to break down.

I recall one particular time when I was in a state of depression because I was going through a divorce. The pressure of the divorce was beginning to weigh on my body. I began to develop physical and mental weakness.

I lost a lot of weight, and I couldn't think straight at times. I felt as if I was having a mental breakdown because my husband had left me to raise two little boys. I didn't have a job or any kind of work experience.

You see, when we got married right out of high school, the plan was that he would work while I stayed home with our children. Well, sometimes things don't always turn out the way you planned them.

I began to have hate myself because I hadn't gone on to college like many of my friends. Neither had I worked a job. Therefore, I had to result to welfare. That was the worst thing I ever had to do.

You see, I had gotten used to living a certain type of way. We had the nice house and car. My life was very comfortable financially. Now, I had to depend on the system to take care of me and my boys. The money I received was barely enough to pay the rent and bills. I felt helpless, what was I to do. My life was turned upside down. I was wounded emotionally.

I felted abandon, helpless, and neglected. I was in so much pain. I felted as if I had fallen and couldn't get up. How many know that a fall is never fun, but the good news is that you can rebound from a fall?

You see, most of us look at pain as being a negative thing, but there can also be some positivity in your pain. Sometimes, there's power in your pain. Sometimes, pain will make you run and get some help. That's exactly what I did. I ran and got some help from God.

You see, it's easy to give up and give in to the pressures of life. It's easy to give up and give in to discouragement and defeat. But that's not what God wants us to do. He wants us to keep our eyes on him because that's where our strength to endure comes from.

Nothing is permanent in this world, not even our troubles. Because when we finally cast our cares on God, the load will begin to get a little lighter. Then one day our troubles just disappear.

Then the next thing you know, we begin to tell people about how good God has been to us because he delivered us from all of our troubles. I am a witness that he will do it.

So yes, you can rebound after a fall because God is not through with you. He still has a blessing for you. He wants to give you a peace that surpasses all understanding. He wants to bless you so that you can be a blessing to others.

So it's time to rejoice again. It's time to rejoice and put your hope in God. When our hope is in God, it makes a difference in how we live in this world. It makes a difference no matter what we do.

You see, there comes a time in our lives when we've done everything we know to do. When we get to that point, we need to stop and give it over to God. Stop worrying about it because he will take care of it. Again, I am a witness.

I lived through the hurts and the pain, the shame and the guilt. I had nothing left but God. He was my peace, my provider, my help, and my friend. He restored me from the death of divorce.

Because some things in me died during my divorce.

But God restored everything I lost during my divorce. He restored my mind and my health. He gave me back my self-esteem. I became free of self-doubt. I started to believe in myself like never before. And now I have peace and joy.

Yes, I rebounded after a fall because after my divorce and knowing that I couldn't live off the money that I was getting from welfare, with the help of God, I was able to find a job. A good job. I went from welfare to faring well.

There Is a Reward after This

Kimberly McWilliams

I remember the day I was cleaning the staff kitchen of the jail I was incarcerated in. I had already served eight months of my time and, yet, this particular day seemed to be the hardest day ever. My heart was so heavy, and with each move of the mop, the tears fell down my face more and more. It got to the place I could barely see what I was doing. I remember throwing my head back, looking up at the ceiling and asking God, "Do you hate me?"

Have you ever been in a place where you felt like, *Lord where are you? I'm in this, and God, when are you going to get me out?* There are periods in our lives that really come to be a test of our patience and our faith. The Bible reads in James 1:2-4 NKJV, "My brethren, count it all joy when you fall into various trials, knowing that the testing of your faith produces patience. But let patience have its perfect work, that you may be perfect and complete, lacking nothing." When I first read that scripture, I was like, *Count it joy when I'm going through? Are you kidding me?* But when I really thought about it, I considered a few things the scripture might be telling me.

1. The joy of the Lord is our strength. When you are in a hard place in your life, it's hard to find joy in it. However, this is the very place the enemy would desire to keep you because he knows if you give up your joy, there goes your strength. To stay weakened allows our "go through" to command our lives. It will govern our thoughts and, in turn, our actions. We find ourselves giving up and believe nothing will ever work out for us. Oh, how far from the truth that is. Maintaining your joy in your go through will guarantee your exit out. Why? Because we will have the strength to stand even when we feel like we're falling. I started off telling you about one of the weakest points in my life. Being incarcerated was not an easy thing. I was separated from my loved ones, and I felt as if I had lost my life. At that point, I had. If I had stayed in that mindset, the time I had to do would have been awful, to the point where I could have lost my mind. Can I tell you the same thing that I told myself at that time? You have come too far to give up now. You've been through before and will come out again. This will not kill you. This will not take you out. You are stronger than you realize. This is now your moment to realize your strength. It's not until we face the storms of life that we really come to see the depths of our strength.

2. The second thing is there is power in patience. Now, I already know you are reading this saying, how can there be power in me waiting. That's the first thing we think about when we hear the word patience. Oh, now I must wait again. And we're right because patience does ultimately mean to wait, but that's not all its asking. It's also asking you to trust. That's the root of why we don't want to wait because we fear trusting. To wait on an answer means we trust one is on the way. When you decide to be patient, you make the decision to have the power to trust. Your posture is saying that I trust it even when I don't see it simply because God said it. Patience increases your faith. It restores your hope that everything really will be all right, in due time. That the battles I face, I will not lose. That while it seems like I'm losing, really, I'm still winning. Patience causes you to declare and decree things over your life and every area concerning you. The Bible says that life and death lie in the power (there goes that word again) of our tongue. We have the authority to give life to, or take life from, our situations. Every good thing, I declare I shall have. The bad, I decree must go. Stop right now and just begin to declare I shall have what God says I shall have. I will be who God says I will be. I will do what God says I will do. I am more than a conqueror through Him. I am victorious.

3. Lastly, there is a reward at the end of this. I know this will sound strange, but what would

have seemed to be the worst time of my life ended up being one of the best things to happen to me. On the outside, by appearances, I was living a good life. What people didn't know was I was struggling in my finances, my ministry, and in my relationship. I had dealt with so much rejection in my life that I was presently with a man who treated me like anything. I loved him with my everything, and in return, I wondered if he even liked me at times. It got so bad that I found myself compromising just to get any attention from him. I lost sight of what was important and eventually lost sight of myself. The path I was on was leading me to that place called nowhere. I'm reminded, even as I type, the God we serve always provides a way of escape. I'm so glad about it. So, I'm sure you're asking, "Kim, that was your way of escape?" Yes, the time I served provided my way of escape. All my life, I lived it trying to be who I thought everyone else wanted me to be. I never came to know who I was for myself. Even present day, I'm still discovering who I am and what makes me happy. For many of us, we compromise ourselves for the benefit of others, to the place we stop existing. We get so good at faking happiness, we become numb to the life we are living of misery. That's not the existence destined for us. It took me to go away to finally realize that. Can I tell you, as you are reading this, that your life matters? You're not just existing to live for everyone and everything else.

You're existing because God created you for a specific purpose. That his plans for you are for the good and that you should prosper.

Today is not the day for you to die in your go through. There is so much ahead of you that you will never come to realize if you stop right here. Once upon a time, I believed life would be better without me, but I'm so glad fairy tales end with a happily ever after. Let me end with telling you what happened in the kitchen that day. While cleaning, the door to the kitchen opened and in walked a deputy. Lunch time was over, so I really didn't know why they were coming in. Can I tell you a divine set up was in store for me. I told the deputy lunch was over, and before they walked out the door, they turned and said to me, "I got a call from Ms. Brown, and you are approved for the program." At first, I had no idea what they were talking about, but then it hit me. I WAS APPROVED! See, there was this work release program I wanted to get into that would allow me a little freedom while I completed my time. In addition, and most importantly, I could see my family. I failed to mention earlier that my son was only 9 days old when I got locked up. Certainly, it hurt to see my newborn and not be able to touch him or my daughter, who was 7, at the time. In my attempt to get in the program before, I was told no. I was getting discouraged and ready to give up, but my faith wouldn't let me waver. I let patience have its perfect work, and now, I was receiving reward on the other side. Sure, it didn't come when I would have liked, yet it was still on time. See, there had to be a delay because if it happened when I wanted, I never would have learned nor come to trust the way I had. The delays in life don't come to hurt; they really come to help and, at times, heal. Might I declare, this is your recovery moment. Take back your joy, your peace, strength, clarity, love, hope, and sound mind. For the trials you face today, you won't see tomorrow if you only believe.

Girl, now is your time to get up and win! There is a reward after this.

Prepare to Participate in Your Good Life

Meshelle Merritt

You are enough. You have the time, energy, and resources to do what God purposes you to do! Have you decided that you are going to WIN? Early in life, my father gave me this advice, "Stay away from stupid people and negative people." With God's words and my earthly father's words, I can firmly say, "I will not be denied!" Now, I need you to repeat that to yourself, write it on your bathroom mirror, and keep those thoughts with you for the rest of your life.

The next step is to define who you are. What are your limits? What will you tolerate and not tolerate? What is your life philosophy? What are your personal standards? What are your family standards? Most importantly, what is God's purpose for your life? This writing is to give you some information and tactics for success.

Readers are leaders, and I read one book per week—not to be an intellectual but to understand how people, things, and culture are coming at me. Are you a victim? Well, there is this thing called

"Constructive Knowledge," which states you are responsible for knowing whether you know it or not. We've all heard the joke that states if you want to hide a million dollars from a man put it in a book. This is why it is important to read. As a personal habit, I only read non-fiction (mainly books on leadership, management, technology, and business). I'm offering information to help you make your life plan, so make a plan with the end in mind. Knowledge is power, but in this Age of Information, if you don't know, people don't have time for you. If you can Google or YouTube the subject and you didn't, people will become dismissive of you.

Spirit / Spiritual Warfare

Read "The Good Book." You'll never know God's will for your life until you know His Word; this is why it is important to read The Holy Bible. Did you know that you can get through the New Testament in four days via audiobook and the Old Testament in two weeks by the same method? You can. Do it!

Protect and make constant decision regarding everything listed in this box.

God	Spirit	Holy Spirit	Time
Self	Soul	Salvation	Energy
Family	Body	Physical Health	Resources
Career	Mind	Mental Health	Money

Live a clean life and remember the more you do wrong the less freedom you will have. Learn from other people's mistakes!

Listen to the Holy Spirit. Wisdom will come as you go through The Holy Bible. Wisdom also comes from learning from other people's mistakes. Make good decisions! A good life comes from making good choices and quality decisions. Do you know how to pray? Learn how to! Are you ready for spiritual warfare? If not, prepare for battle. What does your materialism look like and is that materialism useful or harmful to you? What do you idolize? Are you being manipulated by people and things? If you can clearly define and say "Yes" to these questions, you're well on your way to setting your life on a good path.

Are you worried about finances all the time? At an early age, I was told, "If you don't have cash, have credit, and if you don't have credit, have cash." The reality is today you need cash, good personal credit, and good business credit. If you have a hang-up about money, study on finance and business management. Learn how to build wealth and keep wealth, that way you won't have to be a jerk about money. Listed below is "Maslow's Hierarchy of Needs" for you to use as a guideline to build your Life Plan and Budget needs as you achieve each level.

Maslow's Hierarchy of Needs [Psychology 101]
- Self-Actualization [Work Plan, Education, Employment/Career]
- Esteem Needs
- Love/Belonging [Family/Church/Community]

- Safety Needs
  [Housing/Transportation/Behavioral
  Health/Healthcare/Activity of Daily Living]
- Physiological Needs [Breathing, Food, Water,
  Warmth, Sleep, Shelter, Excretion, Clothing]

My observation is most black people's relationship with capitalism is unhealthy. America is a capitalistic society and always needs low wage workers until automation and AI take those jobs away completely. Some of the most aggressive and disrupting technologies are being developed that will make fast food jobs obsolete. Learn about computer engineering and be able to understand coding, such as JAVA or C/C#. It doesn't take long, and it could lead to high paying employment opportunities without earning a college degree. Allow yourself to be flexible and learn a lot about many different areas and master one. It's called agility, and you need it for today's business climate.

Forty years ago in the Industrial Era, people could expect to work for the same company for their entire working life. In the Information Age, people are completing their education about 10 years earlier, entering into the job market sooner at a six-figure or higher income, pushing to become millionaires with passive income, and retiring earlier. If you are not personally able to participate at a high-level, you will be left behind quickly. You are going to be further behind if you don't understand what I am explaining to you, and you will be standing still while others are progressing further and building momentum. The historical timeline of achievement was about 23 years old. With the rapid change because of a greater access

215

to information, it is now 13 years to complete high school, 16 to complete undergrad, and 18 to finish master's degrees. The evolution of change is making the current timeline of achievement quicker for well supported individuals with access to the right technology.

Technology is the equalizer to success, and it is the disrupter to past success. Your personal assignment is to develop a plan for success quickly and close the gap for yourself and those around you. It's the pathway to big dollars. Look on job websites that specialize in six-figure incomes and find a career that you like. Backwards plan on how to educate yourself to be qualified for that position and execute it!

- Determine the education needed. Online, technology school, or college degree.
- Get to a six-figure income as soon as possible and grow so that money is no longer an issue.
- Look and listen to what successful people are doing.

A few specific careers to research are Professional Project Management (PMP), Supply Chain Management, and Computer Information Security Auditor (CISA). You can study and get into well-paying jobs in a short period of time in these fields.

This is a special note to black men because as I've gone through my education and career, rarely do I see black men, and I wonder where they are. The state of the American culture is in a precipitous decline, and black men are falling prey to the deception and getting blamed for some of the decay. Every culture knows that part of a man's wealth development is marriage, but black men delay partnering with someone good to their demise. They should meet, court, and marry as soon as possible with their families' guidance. I would almost suggest arranging marriages because of the statistical information regarding black marriages. Everyone's goal is to protect their dignity, reputation, integrity, and influence. Protect your image and "Dress for Success." This isn't in anyway referring to street creditability, pride, or thugging. I'm referring to the business success! A real boss is always a legal and well-respected business man.

To all people, I will say that opportunity abounds for those prepared to participate. The good news is it's easier than ever, and becoming prepared to participate is fun and rewarding. People not prepared to participate will be unmarketable and relegated to unskilled, low-paying jobs until they figure a way to automate their position.

In closing, I'm challenging you to make decisions for yourself so you can have a bright and happy future.

Plan it Out, Act It Out -> Don't Be a Victim

- Make a Life Plan.
- Read the Holy Bible.
- Stay away from stupid people and negative people.
- Keep a reading list of books you've read and re-read them when necessary.
- Make a Life Plan.
- Execute the Plan.
- Pass on the information and help others.

Pushing Past Obstacles to Reach Your Destiny

Tracy Palmer

Life has a way of throwing delays, denials, stumbling blocks, sicknesses, hurts, and betrayals at us. Some of which maybe our own fault by way of bad decision making, some happens at the hands of others, some may be the environment in which we grew up in, and some are just simply "LIFE HAPPENING." Over the years, I've had to tell myself, "Girl, Get Up and Win."

As a child, teenager, or women, we all dream big, have great plans, visions and dreams, we even hear from God, but sometimes doubt him, we settle for less, we get stuck in our depressed state of what life has thrown our way, we listen to the negativity of self-talk from people we share our dreams and visions with, many of us may live and operate in the dysfunction that we have grown up in, or we just simply give up and throw in the towel, but I am reminded of *Philippians 4:13, "I can do all things through Christ who strengthens me."*

This scripture should be a reminder to say to self or other, "Girl, Get Up and Win."

For me coming from young teenage parents, my father was an alcoholic and abusive, they had a dysfunctional marriage at a very young age, and both were high school dropouts, I witnessed a lot of dysfunctional behaviors that I found out later on in life were not functional, but had attached to me as a young girl. I was mimicking many of the same behaviors I witnessed as a child; heartbreak, betrayal, sickness, failed relationships, alcoholism, and abusive relationships. I realized that all the negative dysfunctional behaviors of my childhood life followed me to my teenage life and would grow in my adult life as I displayed a lot of what I witnessed as a child. One would say that was a generational curse. I found myself with failed relationships, bad decision making, and not seeing myself grow or fulfill any of the dreams I had because I felt I came from a poverty place; therefore, I had a poverty mindset.

As a child, I had dreams of becoming a schoolteacher, and I had enlisted into the military my senior year of high school, but when I found out I was pregnant, I dropped out of high school and did not go into the military because I didn't understand the terminology the recruiter was using as he explained to me the process when you are pregnant. I did not realize until I became older that the reason I wanted to be a teacher was because I wanted to help children who came from an environment that looked like or had similarities to the environment I came from. I wanted to help them, not even realizing I needed help and deliverance before I could help anyone else.

One day I questioned God, I got mad at God, and I wanted to know how long would I have to endure the abuse, failures, heartbreaks, and betrayals that I was going through. While I laid around and pitied with woe why me, I had lost focus on the dreams, plans, and visions I had. Meanwhile, my plan became delayed because I was in a state of mind that I could no longer focus on what was important. It seemed to me everything around me was falling apart, and I did not have anyone who could help me get on track.

So, one day I decided to open my bible and began to read in ***Habakkuk 2:2, "And the Lord answered me, and said, write the vision, and make it plain upon tables, that he may run that readeth it."*** That stuck with me, and in that moment, I understood regardless of what I was going through, life had to go on in spite of what I felt; the dream, the plan, and vision I had needed to be written out so that others could read it and run with it. I began putting the pen to the paper. I started researching information that was going to be beneficial to what I wanted to do with my life. Now that I am an adult, I had to forgive, let some things go, and move on. People do not understand how "UN-FORGIVENESS" will keep you in a place of unstableness. Even though you might think you are growing, your true growth doesn't come until you are "FREE."

I began journaling, and journaling became a way for me to release negative feelings, emotions, and thoughts. At the same time, journaling was giving me a peace of mind and a mind to tell myself, "Girl, Get Up and Win." All those negative things that were hindering me from "getting up and winning" I learned to redirect to a positive place. I learned how to pray and seek the face of God. I wrote it all down; I started analyzing me, changing myself for the good, aligning up my thoughts with the word of God. I was determined to fulfill my purpose. I was not going to die in my process. I realized the process I had to go through was taking me to the purpose God had for my life in order for me to get to my destiny.

It is imperative to surround yourself with people who will push you, pray for you and with you, and help you get on track to win. Too many times, we have people in our circles who seem to think that these places are where winning takes place: Depressed Dr., Jealousy Junction, Restless Rd., Low Self-Esteem Lane, Doubting Dr., Troubled Terr., Drama Dr., Confusion Court, Hurt Alley, Lying Lane, and Betrayal Blvd. "Girl, Get Up and Win!" You are a true winner! You can be whatever you want to be if your faith is strong, you trust God, you pray fervently, and you have a support group who will push you past the painful places that have happened in your life.

Change the things that you can change that are keeping you in a stagnant place. In order to win, you have to be practicing that which you are trying to perfect. Spend time and study that which you are going to win. It could be your job, business, ministry, or a relationship. "Girl, Get Up and Win" is a slogan full of action words, meaning you have to do something to win. The first thing is identify who the subject is: "Girl," and then you have to put the action to it, and in this case, you are being commanded to act twice, which is "Get Up" and "Win." Do not allow the things of life to put you in a losing mind frame. Winning is a great feeling. When you win, you celebrate, and celebration is a way of saying something great is happening, an accomplishment, achievement, or milestone.

In conclusion, life will happen, and you will have ups and downs. Learning to navigate through the down times is the key to winning. Without difficulties, struggles, and challenges, winning really wouldn't make much sense. Appreciation goes to another level in you when you learn to persevere through all the things that keep you from winning and be successful in life. Maya Angelou said it best when you stated, **"You may encounter many defeats, but you must not be defeated. In fact, it may be necessary to encounter the defeats, so you can know who you are, what you can rise from, how you can still come out of it."** Now, "Girl, Get Up and Win."

Many blessings to every sister who may not be there yet, but with the help of her positive sisters, she is on her way. It doesn't matter how you get to the *win* at the end; it matters that you just get there.

Girl, Drop It!

Shaletha Sanders

As a child, I enjoyed looking at people, places, and things in magazines. One particular picture I remember viewing had models in Paris walking the runway. My dream one day was to travel to Paris, New York, Los Angeles, and the list goes on. I aspired to have front row seats with my girls and observe a high end fashion show. I imagined this was every girl's dream and would be the trajectory for my life. I was confident that my desires would no longer be dreams but reality. Furthermore, I had high hopes of one day being photographed and featured in a popular magazine. Everything sounded good, except there was one prerequisite, I needed to graduate from high school and be legal. As I matured and grew older, part of that dream came true, and I had the opportunity of traveling around the world.

Years passed, and I did not become a runway model; however, I married my high school sweetheart, and of course, he became the man of my dreams. We laughed together, we had fun together, and we ate together. We were in love, and we enjoyed eating out and spending quality time with each other.

I was always told that food is the key to a man's heart. Well, I believe I excelled in that area because I prepared home-cooked meals daily and did not believe in eating out. I prepared fried chicken that was double dipped in flour and buttermilk. I managed to get a thick coating on the chicken, and when I put it in the fryer, it came out golden brown with a thick layer of crust. It was delicious! It in the midst of preparing my hubby with hearty meals, I started packing on the pounds. In my opinion, men can eat what they want and put on a few pounds; on the other hand, women can eat a little bit of the wrong thing and pack on a lot of pounds. My post marriage weight was getting out of control. I did not attempt to do anything about it because I continued to enjoy food.

A few more years passed, and I was blessed to give birth to two handsome boys. Although they were handsome, I picked up an additional fifty pounds during those pregnancies. I wanted to do something about it, but I did not have the courage to ask for help. My clothes were getting tighter and tighter. I hated shopping because everything in the front was for smaller women, which left the bigger sizes in the back of the store.

My anniversary was approaching, and my husband surprised me and informed me that we were going to Los Angeles. I was super excited, and all I thought about was, "I'm going to Hollywood." We arrived in Los Angeles and visited many attractions. I heard so much about Rodeo Drive and the Hollywood Walk of Fame. I was hoping to run into a celebrity on Rodeo Drive. While on Rodeo Drive, I found a clothing store that had a pair of pants that I adored. I was looking through the rack for my size and had trouble locating it, so I motioned for the clerk to come help me.

"Do you have a size 18/20 in these pants?" I asked.

"No," he replied before he laughed.

"What is so funny?"

"The biggest size we carry is size 10, same as any other store on this strip."

My emotions and feelings were all over the place. I was embarrassed, irritated, agitated, and angry. I thought I was cute up until the clerk informed me that they did not carry "Big Girl" sizes. I felt like a fool in front of the man of my dreams. I promised myself when I returned home I was going to do something about my weight.

Los Angeles was a great getaway, but there was nothing like home. When I returned home, I had a dream that I was in a size 2 or 4 black dress. This was motivation for me, so I started working out and made healthier food choices. I prayed and asked God for motivation, self-control, and determination. I needed motivation as ambition to lose the weight. Self-control was important because it helped me to say no to all of the fatty foods that I desired. Determination was essential because I was resolute to keep pushing until I reached my weight loss goal. With these three components in my mind, I started losing weight. I lost 5 pounds and then 10 pounds. I was losing weight and feeling great. When I reached a weight loss milestone, I celebrated by going to my favorite restaurant. I attempted to eat in moderation, but I could not resist a slice of Oreo cookie cheesecake. It was so delightful! I should have chosen another way to celebrate, such as shopping or purchasing a book because those celebrations turned into extra pounds. Immediately after I celebrated, I returned home, felt bad, jumped on my treadmill, and started running.

In January of 2008, I was running on my treadmill and felt an excruciating pain in my lower right leg. That night, I placed a bag of ice underneath it hoping the swelling would go down. It seemed as if my leg got bigger overnight. I measured my leg, and it read 19 centimeters around the calf area. I couldn't take the pain, so I went to the emergency room and while waiting an African nurse asked to assist me by offering a wheelchair, and she whispered to me that I had a blood clot in my leg. Without hesitation, I Googled "blood clot," and it read, "A blood clot is when your blood does not flow properly." I was petrified! The doctor ran numerous tests, and sure enough, it came back positive for deep vein thrombosis (DVT). I had to stay in the hospital for three days, and then I was released with special orders. The doctor informed me not to sit around but stay mobile. When I arrived home, I did the total opposite and stayed in the bed. I woke up one morning, and my leg was bent like an ostrich when I stood up. My leg was in that condition for two months. I became depressed, sad, and went into isolation. I felt like I was losing my mind. This went on for months, and then one day, I was viewing a national motivational speaker on television, and she was speaking on faith. As long as I have lived, I always believed that God can do anything but fail. That being said, I had faith that God could and would heal me. I began to believe in my heart that I was healed, I began calling on the name of Jesus, and I started stretching my leg forward. It was a miracle! My leg stretched back to normal. I was healed! I started leaping and running through my house in amazement. I knew firsthand that God was a healer.

After giving birth to my daughter, I ate what I wanted and picked up a lot of weight. In fact, I weighed 238 pounds. I waited a few months prior to working out; I started making healthier food selections and lost over 100 pounds, and I have kept it off since 2011. Girl, I dropped it! All praises to God! I went from a size 18/20 to a size 4. God is good! The picture that I saw in my dream with the little black dress was now my reality.

In life, we often desire what we see in a picture; however, we fail to consider the process it takes in order to obtain the results in the picture. For example, I love to bake cookies and cakes and rely on the directions from the recipe and the list of ingredients in the cookbook. If the recipe is followed correctly, and all the ingredients are used, then the finished product will mirror the picture in the cookbook. The process can be messy; however, if the recipe is followed correctly, then the finished product will be delicious. If ingredients are not used or are substituted, then the finished product will be a disaster. With that being said, I went through the weight loss process by selecting healthier foods, such as baked meats, vegetables, fruits, and water. In addition to eating healthy, I stayed on a strict workout regimen by running and walking. This allowed me to reach my weight loss goal. The process was extremely challenging at times; however, my desire was to get into that little black dress that I remembered seeing in my dream. Although I didn't consider the process that I would have to go through, I *made* it through, and the picture of me in that black dress looked absolutely amazing.

Yay! I did it!

Girl, if I dropped it, so can you!

How to Kick Rejection to the Curb and Win

Cutella Talbot

It is often said that life is 10 percent of what happens to you and 90 percent of how you react to it. One day, I sat on the beautiful By Nature Grace Bay Beach in the Turks and Caicos Islands watching the sunset. My heart was filled with sadness, and I cried so much that evening while watching the sun set. I thought, if only my pain and sadness could go down with the sun and never arise again, that would be the happiest day of my life. You see, I was looking for a temporary fix and what I needed was a permanent fix. I wanted the success and everything that comes with it, but I did not want to go through the process because when going through the process, you have to confront issues in the tissues. I had stored up so many years of pain and rejection from my childhood, and these things that happened to me in the past took such a toll on me mentally and emotionally that I would lock myself away in my room for days and never come outside. I thought everyone was out to get me and hurt me, until the day I went back to the beach, and I sat in the sand, that beautiful white sand, and watched the sunset again. This time, my mindset was different. I was ready to let it go, all of it because I realized the world was moving and evolving. Nothing stays the same, and I did not want to stay in the same condition that I was in. I made a conscious decision to let it all go and forgive the people who did me wrong and even myself for locking my gifts and talents in prison. I was ready to kick rejection to the curb and win.

I realized that I had the key to my destiny and God has the key to my purpose. I started believing in myself again, and I reminded myself every day that I am worthy of being all that God had called me to be. I stood to my feet and shouted: I am destined for greatness.

Sometimes, when you find yourself in a hole and you have no one to pull you out, you must find that inner strength to pull yourself through; this is where your inner strength is developed, and you know that you have to do whatever it takes to come forth from that state. Never remain stagnant; there is always better on the other side. You may ask, "How do you know this?" I have been there many times, and today nothing holds me back from accomplishing my goals in life and following my dreams. I wanted better, I wanted a better life, and today, I am living my best life.

I found out that the lack of knowledge always opens the door for experimentation, manipulation, exploitation, and mistakes, particularly when you are at your most vulnerable and challenging circumstances. In critical moments, the questions are "needs versus sacrifice." History would record that brokenness has a great link to trust and emotional problems.

Today, financial independence, sound education, positive goal setting, and self-determination are the keys to accomplishing our far-reaching and everlasting object. Yes, we need to possess the basic survival kit in life to obtain happiness, but we also need to realize that self-love starts within and expresses itself in our relationships. It cannot be built on physical beauty or availability; rather, you demand love because of who you are as self-respect strengthens an everlasting bond.

My message of success is to allow others' accomplishments to be a springboard and pattern for motivation. Oftentimes, imitating successful people leads you to success. As the ladder you climb leads to upward mobility, I caution you never to look back from whence you started, know that every step you make takes you closer to the top. Sometimes on our journey, obstacles find themselves on our path, but God allows obstruction to be our instruction, for without a process, there will never be a success.

Too many sisters have fallen and failed to get up. I learned that dwelling on painful scares of bad memories always delays healing that is promised. Always digest on this true proverb, "There is an end to every beginning, and that too shall pass."

My life had knots that I untied many years later as I didn't know what I know now; therefore, I became an advocate to reveal my story as a classroom lesson. As I introspect over my past, I cried and smiled, not because of the pain or the pleasure, but instead, because I concluded to put a stop sign and to never walk that road again.

As we go through life's journey, don't allow the mishaps of what we didn't do keep up from doing *now*. Don't live in a state of the "I could have, would have, or should have" syndrome. I learned from experience that what I have accomplished is a result of believing in that I can do all things, and by the grace of God, nothing is impossible. I further learned that success is not walking through a rose garden without meeting thorns; it's about overriding fear that always places doubt in utilizing your full potential. I wish to remind all of us that the struggles in life are to make us stronger and more equipped to beat greater battles ahead.

Sisters, we are specially and wonderfully made, powerful and influential in our nation-building. People take us for granted because we refused to exercise the purpose of our existence. It's not a coincident that we are here on this earth. We are equivalent to a *lock and key*; we are needed, and without us, things cannot be complete. I would like to suggest that we take our rightful places in society and make that meaningful contribution to shape, mold, and fashion lives as we go forward. I believe it's not what we can't do, but what we are not doing. We are a force to be reckoned with in every facet of life; let's take our hopes and dreams through and beyond the White House as too many sisters and brothers are suffering and waiting on advocates like ourselves to rise up as freedom fighters.

My story goes on, and this chapter of my life has to move to the next level. When we work, sing, laugh, and link together, everyone rises and smiles with a joy of accomplishment. Success is based on empowerment, love, and how we treat ourselves and others. We are more powerful together than we are apart. The key to getting up is to get up and go after what you want, start by taking small steps to get there, and remember on your way to the top to never take the elevator. Always take the stairs because if you make one mistake on that first step, you will still have time to stand on that first step you took, clean yourself up again, and step forward like nothing ever happened. This is how God does it. When God purifies us, he does it good, and you never look like what you have been through.

Girl, it's time to kick rejection to the curb and win!

A Quick Thank You

Thank you for reading *Girl, Get Up and Win*!

If you enjoyed the book, please take a moment to write a review as your words truly make a difference.

If you purchased your book at Amazon.com, please post your review there, or you can email it to us at info@courageouswomanmag.com and add "Review" in subject line.

For more inspiration for your daily living, please subscribe to *Courageous Woman Magazine* at http://www.courageouswomanmg.com.

If you're interested in joining us as a coauthor for *Girl, Get Up and Win* Volume 2, email us at info@courageouswomanmag.com for more details.

Thank you again!